NO CHOPSTICKS REQUIRED

ADVANCE PRAISE FOR THIS BOOK

'Katrina brilliantly captures all the behind-the-scenes drama of the Beijing Olympics from the Chinese perspective. It was fascinating to discover how China treats its athletes and their cultural views on sport. A wonderful enthralling story that brings Shanghai vividly to life for all to read.'
Dawn Fraser, AO, MBE

'A riveting read!'
Peter FitzSimons, journalist and author of *Kokoda* and *Charles Kingsford Smith and Those Magnificent Men*

'Katrina Beikoff has captured the essence of a thriving, colourful city on a fast moving trajectory, while evoking the day to day challenge of living in a country where the language, culture and habits are as stimulating as they are demanding.'
Pru Goward, State MP for Goulburn

'This is a book which is easy to read, but offers lots to learn. It isn't just a travel memoir, it's an array of insights into culture, parenting, politics, media, epic tragedy and our shared humanity. Weighty topics such as oppression in Tibet and the editorial and ethical perils of journalism in China sit seamlessly alongside more seemingly mundane matters such as living with fireworks and exploring the local food offerings (which turns out not to be so mundane at all). The book's insights into poverty, educational competitiveness and the growing impacts of netizens and the new media show that, like modern day newspapers, things aren't always as black and white as you might think.'
Andrew Bartlett, political and social commentator and former Democrats leader

'A brilliantly written and often hilarious read, Beikoff's *No Chopsticks Required* brings alive the madness, confusion and hilarity of living and working abroad with the added burden of young children. It's a tale which will inspire knowing laughter from fellow ex-pats, and will encourage others to consider subjecting themselves to the exhilarating madness of a stint overseas.'
David Penberthy, senior columnist, News Limited

NO CHOPSTICKS REQUIRED

MY FAMILY'S UNEXPECTED YEAR IN SHANGHAI

KATRINA BEIKOFF

FINCH PUBLISHING

SYDNEY

No Chopsticks Required: My family's unexpected year in Shanghai
First published in 2011 in Australia and New Zealand by Finch Publishing Pty Limited,
ABN 49 057 285 248, Suite 2207, 4 Daydream Street, Warriewood, NSW, 2102, Australia.

12 11   8 7 6 5 4 3 2 1

The National Library of Australia Cataloguing-in-Publication entry:

Beikoff, Katrina, 1969-
No Chopsticks Required : my family's unexpected year in Shanghai/Katrina Beikoff.
9781921462290 (pbk.)

Beikoff, Katrina, 1969
Journalists--Biography.
Shanghai (China)--Social life and customs--21st century.

951.13206

Edited by Abigail Nathan
Editorial assistance by Ron Buck
Text typeset in Berling Roman by Pier Vido
Cover design by Peter Long
Cover image by Ewa Kulon
Printed by McPhersons Printing

Finch titles can be viewed and purchased at **www.finch.com.au**

CONTENTS

Chapter 1   A Great Proposition   *1*

Chapter 2   Shanghai Calling   *7*

Chapter 3   The Big Gulp   *18*

Chapter 4   Early Settlers   *28*

Chapter 5   Lessons in Rivalry   *45*

Chapter 6   Happy New Year   *57*

Chapter 7   Snowed In   *64*

Chapter 8   It's Newspapers, But Not as We Know It   *71*

Chapter 9   The Tibet Situation   *83*

Chapter 10   A Helping Hand   *93*

Chapter 11   A Class of Our Own   *103*

Chapter 12   Behind the Facade   *115*

Chapter 13   Is That Elvis in Emergency?   *125*

Chapter 14   Don't Tell Me Not to Panic   *138*

Chapter 15   May 12, 2008   *144*

Chapter 16   Online Army   *156*

Chapter 17   China's Olympics   *165*

Chapter 18   Here Comes Haibo   *176*

Chapter 19   Milking a Scandal   *183*

Chapter 20   A Dumpling For Every Occasion   *200*

Chapter 21   Who Could Be Cranky at Cinderella?   *216*

Chapter 22   Blue Ants to Bedtime   *224*

Chapter 23   Fear and Timing in Shanghai   *232*

Chapter 24   It Feels Like Home   *239*

Acknowledgements   *250*

To Milly and Nelson, you make everything more fun.
And to Smarty for the promise it would never be dull.

CHAPTER 1

A GREAT PROPOSITION

Vegemite is really hard to remove from the Great Wall of China.

It was meant to be one of life's big moments, the kind they feature in movies of self-satisfied souls ticking off one of the ten things they want to do before they die. I had envisioned myself gazing serenely at the Great Wall, snaking off into the distance. My partner and I would be bathed in dappled sunlight and the golden glow of achievement while acknowledging our great fortune at being atop one of the world's great wonders. Meanwhile, our cherubic offspring would be expressing appropriate awe and appreciation at the amazing location to which their adventurous parents had brought them.

Instead, I had my head down, back-to-the-view, trying to clean Vegemite smushed by a cranky toddler into ancient granite bricks put in place more than 2000 years ago. It wasn't going at all to plan.

As I rubbed and smeared, someone grabbed me by the arm. My heart hammered. Maybe we'd been sprung and were going to be expelled from China for defacing the nation's greatest monument with a salty yeast extract.

But it was a local woman and it appeared she was oblivious to my task. Instead, her husband motioned for her to get nearer, her clutch tightened, and other family members, friends and onlookers closed in. A young boy, perhaps her son, began chanting at me 'Good thank-you, how are you?' on an endless loop. I looked around for my own kids. My daughter was in the middle of another huddle of Chinese tourists, with the flashes and pops of their cameras firing in her direction. My toddler son was still waging his war on sandwich fillings.

My partner seemed to be saying something. It may have been important, but I couldn't hear. I wasn't listening. I knew we should never have stopped for a snack. We'd made the fateful error of novices driving through soft sand: fail to keep moving and you'll be stuck for hours.

And so I turned to my captors with their cameras, and smiled.

I was standing on the Great Wall of China on China's National Day, October 1. The October air was crisp and fresh and the sky a brilliant blue. I didn't expect such a perfect day, but that was one of the benefits of being in and around Beijing in the wake of the city's hosting of the 2008 Olympic Games. The cars and factories around Beijing may just have been given the all clear to resume belching toxins into the atmosphere after the Olympic-time ban, but standing on the Great Wall at Mutianyu I could see nothing but the surprising green of the Chinese bushland speckled with the first blush of autumn.

Mutianyu is one of the prettiest and best preserved sites at which to climb the Great Wall of China which winds about 6700 kilometres from the east to west of the country across desert, grasslands, mountains and plateaus. While a chairlift was available at Mutianyu to take us up into the overlapping mountain ranges and deposit us at one of the wall's turrets, that didn't mean it was possible to avoid early-morning souvenir vendors offering 'I Climbed the Great Wall' T-shirts, fans, swords and 'antiques – made to order'.

Up on the ridge, with the Great Wall of China stretching away before us, its watchtowers jutting skyward like spikes on a dragon's back, the view was everything I could hope for. But the crowd wasn't. This was to be no blissful stroll along one of the world's great wonders, pausing to marvel at the scenery and watch my family enjoy this special moment. Rather, we were caught like flotsam, swept along in the flow of eager Chinese sightseers, determined to capture every aspect of the experience.

China, with one quarter of the world's population, is all about people. October 1 is in the middle of a week-long holiday or 'Golden Week' for all Chinese workers. Chinese people on holiday don't mind a crowd and don't want to miss a thing. It seemed thousands of Chinese had chosen the same day as us to shatter the calm at Mutianyu. I figured that I shouldn't be bothered by this. It was so typical of our year in China.

It was a year in which we had been constantly overwhelmed, especially by the enormity of numbers in China. We'd lived a life so alien to what we were accustomed to in Australia, had changed so much in our understanding of the East and learned to value so many of the things we take for granted. As a family we had also become even closer, often just trying to make it through each day amid the peculiar challenges of living in a Chinese city. And we'd had to adapt, for in China our expectations and the reality we encountered rarely seemed to match.

It had been a year that had torn us from our comfort zones. We'd eaten snakes and frogs and chicken feet and learned to quite like tea. We'd altered our ideas of achievement to being able to last 24 hours without suffering a major cross-cultural mix-up, facing death in a taxi, or being caught having to use a public toilet. We had at times questioned our wisdom in bringing our two small children to China, but ultimately delighted in the ability of the kids to thrive and even pick up some of the local language and customs. We'd even wondered if we ever really wanted to go back home.

We had been lucky to be able to visit places like the Great Wall of China and live in one of the most exciting and cosmopolitan metropolises on the planet, despite anticipating Shanghai, with a population roughly the same as Australia, to be a city struggling under the weight of its own population and offering only the most basic services and comforts. But Shanghai, for all its pollution and overcrowding and grime, had proved to be stimulating beyond compare and its people proud, pushy and idiosyncratic. We'd been able to meet and befriend vibrant and informed locals, even though China remains a tightly controlled society where access to information is restricted and openly expressing ideas still risks punishment by the Communist Party. As expats, we'd also been able to experience the benefits, difficulties and suspicions of living as outsiders in a foreign land. Through my job, I'd learned that the media in China is vastly different to journalism as we know it in the West, and that my hopes of witnessing a shift to a freer press in the 'new China' was still a way off. And perhaps the most refreshing – and frustrating – discovery had been that even with so many advances in technology, travel and business that threaten to make the world a more homogeneous place, there are still massive and baffling differences between Chinese and foreigners, and that there will always remain a chasm between East and West.

On the Great Wall of China, as I tried to hide the Vegemite stain and remain upright while my son, who by now had thrown all of his snacks off the Great Wall and had begun to wend through my legs to avoid the crushing masses, I realised that much of the joy of our time in China was the utter chaos and challenge of daily life. I never failed to be surprised.

I looked to my daughter, by now well-practised in posing for cameras, whose blonde hair was poking out of a Minnie Mouse hat I could just see off to my right. She was holding hands and hugging local children to the delight of the crowds.

And I sought out my partner, unable to suppress a grin at the craziness of our morning.

He was still talking.

'Were you listening?' he demanded.

'Yes,' I lied.

'I asked if you ever thought that we would get to be here. And now that we are ... will you marry me?'

Ah, one of life's big moments. I was to get my movie scene atop the Great Wall of China. I had nearly missed it.

'No, I never thought we would be so lucky to visit China, let alone live in Shanghai. But I'm so glad we have. It has been one of the greatest years of my life.' And I said 'yes'.

CHAPTER 2

SHANGHAI CALLING

'Do you want to go to China?'

It was one of the more unusual ways to wake up to a warm winter's day on Queensland's Gold Coast.

It was August, and there was a bit of a chill in the salty air, but I was already thinking of ducking down to the beach. We could all have a swim at our sheltered little estuary before a pancake breakfast overlooking the surfing action, then wander leisurely back home along the ocean foreshore, letting the kids have a play in the park.

I ignored the question. It hardly fit with my morning's plans.

We had been at the Gold Coast for about 18 months. We had been settling. After five moves in five years, it was time to stop, to take a breath.

We had found a location we loved. I never thought I would be living at the Gold Coast, one of Australia's tourism hotspots and a surfing mecca with 57 kilometres of pristine beaches backed up by a delightfully underdeveloped hinterland about an hour's drive south of the state capital of Brisbane. The Gold Coast has long been a lure for southerners fleeing the colder climates of Victoria and New South Wales who come to Queensland for a holiday and then find they can't bear to leave. I did not picture myself as one of those Gold Coasters – I was born in Queensland after all. But within the past five years I had moved from Sydney to Canberra and then to Brisbane. After leaving Sydney, none of the moves ever felt quite right. And so I had plumped for yet another move, to the Gold Coast. Now, with two young children – Matilda, aged three, and one-year-old Nelson – it was time for the family to pick a spot and, well, stick.

My partner and I were hoping it was finally time for us to let our lives becalm after meeting in Sydney while we were both employed as journalists in the same newspaper bureau covering the 2000 Sydney Olympic Games. It is perhaps infantile, or perhaps it comes from our time spent working together in a newsroom, but I have never been able to graduate from calling Gary by his nickname of Smarty – coined using that ever-so-Australian habit of adding a 'y' to a surname. When I garnered a prized gig in the sports department at Sydney's *Daily Telegraph* following the Olympic Games, I continued working with Smarty and leaning on his experience as a long-time sports editor for professional advice. Our relationship changed course, as did my career, just before I left Sydney and sports writing two years later to take up a position as a media and political advisor in Canberra. We maintained a long-distance relationship as I was based in the Australian capital and Smarty had returned after the Olympics to living and working in Brisbane. The nature of the relationship changed course again when my boss in Canberra, the former leader of the Australian Democrats Senator Andrew Bartlett, ran into some problems requiring around-the-clock crisis management for the Party in December 2003. In another big upheaval, Mark Latham defeated Kim Beazley for the leadership of the Australian Labor Party, fuelling expectations then Prime Minister John Howard would call an election in early 2004. I was feeling particularly exhausted by this turn of events by the end of December and found myself struggling to summon the energy to dive into a federal election campaign. Then I found out I wasn't just tired. I was pregnant.

Smarty seemed quite pleased when I announced I'd quit my job and was coming to Brisbane to live with him. He also didn't seem to mind a bit when I proposed renovating his house because we were going to have a baby. For the next few months we floated in a kind of delirium and spent our time marvelling at our unexpected good fortune and the ridiculously tiny lemon bunny suit laid out in the spare room that would soon be filled by our little baby. It was an especially sweet time as I had previously resigned myself to never having children and thought my career would have to be the focus of my existence. Smarty too thought he had missed his chance to become a dad. When Matilda May was born in July, it was a happier, more surprising and fulfilling moment than I could ever have imagined. She completely changed our lives.

With Matilda, whom we call Milly, the centre of our world, we agreed the time had come to shelve our mutual practice of avoiding anything resembling a plan, and think about our future as a family. One of the things we really wanted for our daughter, we decided, was to have her grow up enjoying the best environment we could provide with fresh air, open space and a beach. And so, with my urging, Smarty quit his job in Brisbane to take up a post as editor of a small newspaper on the Queensland–New South Wales border, and we moved to the Gold Coast. I contributed to the changes by revealing on Milly's first birthday that I was pregnant again. It seemed we weren't very good at planning after all. Our beautiful baby boy, Nelson, was born at the Gold Coast in March. Our family was complete.

We soon found a house we could call ours in a suburban pocket on the southern end of the Coast, close to the beach, parks and a lake. A school we were eyeing for our kids was within walking distance, and their playgroup, the library, dance and music classes, and a pool for swimming lessons were all close by. I was already planning which surf club we would join so the children could get into junior life-savers, or nippers, when they were old enough and checking out sports ovals and stadiums ahead of our battle over whether the kids would play basketball, Australian Rules football, or both.

We had the lifestyle we had sought – days that revolved largely around the beach and parks, our friends and our kids' friends. We had work almost under control. Smarty was enjoying editing the local paper. After spending years as the sports editor of the state's

largest daily, he was feeling his decision to go full tilt at the
newspaper business and seek an editorship was paying off. It had
been a difficult slog to bring the small daily up to a higher standard,
but he was enjoying the challenge and felt he was making headway
with the paper as well as infusing new enthusiasm for the task into
the staff.

I'd started emerging from my mummy cocoon. I was taking on a
little freelance writing and a weekly column. I realised I had no
desire to head back to a metropolitan newsroom, nor back into the
political fray, for a while yet. It was the correct decision – I was
having better luck recalling the little known second verse of 'Jack
and Jill' than the second in charge of the Australian Democrats. I
was loving just looking after the kids and making my little writing
contributions. We were actually getting into a bit of a groove.

'No, I don't want to go to China,' I finally said. 'Give me one
reason why we should leave all this.'

'I know. Just thought I'd ask,' Smarty said, then smiled and closed
his eyes.

Kevin Rudd famously lived in China. Much has been made of the
Mandarin-speaking former Australian Prime Minister and his links
and affinity with Beijing. But mainly, I remember his story about the
rats. In an article by Christine Jackman in The *Weekend Australian*
before his 2007 election victory, Rudd describes the assault on his
young family by the beasts of Beijing. They had worked tirelessly to
break down his defences, and the young diplomat had reached a
point where he felt he had no option but to resort to uncharacteristic
heavy handedness to convince his foes to vacate the area both he
and they felt entitled to inhabit. Finally, feeling all other avenues of

persuasion had been exhausted, a pyjama-clad Rudd armed himself with a souvenir nulla-nulla (Aboriginal fighting stick) and in the middle of the night, aided and abetted by wife Therese Rein, leapt from the bed and clobbered a Beijing rat 'the size of an Australian tabby', cracking its skull. Nice. Let's live there.

A couple of weeks after his mysterious questions about moving to China, Smarty called me from work. I was at the crucial stirring stage of playdough-making and not really up for the interruption.

'Do you remember me asking you about China?' he said. 'I've just had a call from Shanghai and they're interested in us going to work there. We would be what are called "foreign experts".'

Smarty told me the Shanghai seed had been planted at a celebration in early August for the twenty-fifth anniversary of the launch of the *Daily Sun* newspaper in Brisbane. The first editor, John Hartigan – now chairman and chief executive of News Limited – made a noteworthy appearance as guest of honour along with most of the staff from the launch issue. But the most significant conversation of the night, which occurred in the later stages of the evening – and Smarty could therefore be forgiven for forgetting much of it – involved a former colleague who said he had a mate seeking experienced journalists in Shanghai. He wanted to know if anybody was interested. Smarty said he wasn't sure if or why he'd shown interest. But now Shanghai was calling.

I decided to placate Smarty and return the call he'd received from China. I spoke to Sarah Macklin, a 'foreign expert' at the *Shanghai Daily* newspaper and the wife of Bernie Leo, the mate-of-the-mate, chief sub-editor and special advisor to the editor in chief of the Chinese paper. Sarah spoke of Shanghai glowingly. 'Trust me, you'll never want to leave,' she said. It was one of those conversations you later have trouble describing. In the space of 12 minutes, I think I'd pretty much agreed we'd go to China.

'Do you really want to go to China?' I asked Smarty that night, just a little terrified.

'Why? Do you actually want to go?' he responded.

'I don't know, but I think I've said we're going and they might be expecting us in January.'

We didn't really know what to do, so in our tried and tested response to life's big questions, we agreed to worry about it later. I called a former newspaper colleague of mine who had worked for some time in China. He said he'd worked in Beijing and became quite proficient at ping-pong. He said we should go. I considered calling Kevin Rudd, but I wasn't sure I'd get past the Prime Ministerial personal assistants. And he might scare me again with his story about the rats.

Finally, Smarty and I agreed to make lists of pros and cons. We got nowhere with the pros, so started with the cons. It would be an upheaval, there would be pollution, we would get sick, we would both have to work full-time, we'd be arriving in the middle of a freezing winter and we didn't speak Mandarin. Top of the list though, was that the decision wasn't just about us. We had children to consider. We'd specifically chosen not to raise them in a big city. We would also have to leave them with a virtual stranger while we were at work, which could be an ordeal for them, and would certainly be for me as I'd barely even left them alone with their grandparents before. There might also be giant rodents. There was a fairly substantial list of reasons not to go. We let it rest.

But neither of us could shake thoughts of China. The potential Sino sojourn infiltrated my thinking even when I was concentrating on far greater concerns – like my plans to strut my post-baby body at the beach by Christmas. To get past feeling like a rolling sack of spuds every time I encountered the bikini babes at the beach, I had embarked on a fitness program just after Nelson's first birthday. It involved getting up ridiculously early, despite the children not yet sleeping thought the night, and heading to Burleigh Beach where I joined a council-sponsored walking group. We would walk together carrying home-made hand weights of 600 millilitre water bottles that had been filled with sand, and survey the Coast's plethora of super slim, surgically enhanced model-types who passed us wired to their iPods and carrying fancier, far more expensive hand weights. The exercise group also gave me the chance to begin the day smelling the mingled scents of sea salt and sweet pine from the towering Norfolk Pine trees that lined the Burleigh foreshore, and catch those magic moments when dolphins leapt from the waves to greet the new day. It was my own little indulgence and helped clear my head for a day of inevitable child rearing chaos.

On one of those perfect mornings in late September, sweaty-faced from power walking, I made it to the Burleigh Heads lookout where some early-morning types had gathered to catch sight of the last Humpback whales migrating back to colder southern waters. I looked out to sea and thought of China. I couldn't think of the last time I'd knocked back a real opportunity to do something new or different. I couldn't bear the idea that ignorance or fear would prevent me from taking a chance. And I wanted the children to be adventurous and brave and develop the same love of travel that had taken Smarty and me to various parts of the world earlier in our lives. I knew our lopsided list was irrelevant. There was only one reason that we should go to China.

I went home and found Smarty trying to make pancakes from scratch. The kids weren't impressed. He'd used salt instead of sugar. I took the bowl away. The look on my face must have belied the importance of the message I was about to impart.

'We have to go to China,' I said.

'I know,' Smarty replied. 'If we don't, we'll always regret it.'

My thinking exactly.

Many of our friends and family congratulated us on our decision to uproot our lives and take ourselves and the kids off on a bold journey to a far-away land. They also seemed to expect we'd done quite a bit of research on our destination. I knew that part of the process was probably up to me, especially given all the concerns I had over how the children would cope, but for some reason I stalled. It was like I was being overloaded with questions and concerns and demands for emergency strategies and action plans. I almost didn't want to know what we were heading into. I figured we knew so little about Shanghai that it was pointless worrying too much until we actually got there.

The hard part for Smarty and me had been making the big picture decision to go. In our minds, part of that choice meant backing ourselves to deal with whatever issues we encountered. Neither of us wanted to get bogged down in details. I think we feared it might take some of the gloss off our big family adventure. Indiana Jones didn't arrive in Shanghai in the opening sequence of the *Temple of Doom* with suitcases laden with the comforts of home, bags of antiseptic hand gel and an attitude that he'd bail at the first sign of danger. This cinematic image of Shanghai was our dominant vision of the city and we were going to jump in boots and all. Our impression of the city was taken not only from film but novel portrayals of it in its golden era of the 1920s and '30s when Shanghai was known as 'Paris of the East', or less charmingly as the 'Whore of the Orient'. We pictured the city as vibrant and alluring, pulsing with glamour, riches, opulence, and just a touch of menace. We had visions of bustling streets, exotic and mysterious women in silk and cheongsam, parasols and race tracks and colour. There would be jazz and rooms dense with opium smoke and steam from perpetually-bubbling pots of rice and dumplings. We would mix with foreign devils who had descended on this melting pot of the East and who lived in massive mansions and enjoyed a life of decadence while the seedy and unruly back alleys of the city were ruled by gangsters and whip-smart hustlers who thrived on a deal in a city where almost anything goes, especially if it meant money was to be made.

We knew, of course, that this was indeed a shockingly shallow understanding of the city and that post-1930s Shanghai couldn't live up to the stylised intrigue of its 1930s heyday, especially given the massive changes wrought on the city since the Communist Party came to power in 1949. But it was enough. We were going. Someone actually had to get us there. I eventually had to shake off my inertia and focus on at least some of the really important things.

'Do they have spaghetti in Shanghai?' I asked Bernie on one of the many calls he made to us in Australia to check if we were still coming to Shanghai. 'Do they have olive oil, cereal, nappies? And do I really have to bring a year's supply of new bras because the Chinese don't stock larger than a B cup?' Bernie and Sarah had told me to check with them if I had any questions. I'm sure they were regretting their offer.

But we were definitely going. Milly proudly informed her playmates that she was off to China and they would have to ask their mums if they wanted to come and visit. Like her parents, she was struggling to really grasp the extent of the move. I tried explaining to the children that we probably wouldn't see their friends or a beach for a while because we were moving to a big city across the sea that was full of cars and tall buildings and lots and lots of people. Milly had always loved a holiday, especially if it was in a hotel with a lift, and was very excited at the prospect of going to live somewhere that was full of tall buildings. Nelson, who counted 'car' among the first words he ever uttered, seemed reasonably pleased with the explanation as well. As we drove along the esplanade at Currumbin looking across the curve of the coast to the Gold Coast's famous Surfers Paradise skyline one day, Milly enthusiastically informed me that she could actually see China – across the sea and full of tall buildings. When it came to China, I figured we were all clueless, but happy.

I still had no idea what to take as I began bundling together a few boxes to ship to Shanghai containing the necessities for our new life. I packed winter clothes borrowed from friends and bought after desperately scouring the Queensland sales, English language story books, bras, and a first aid kit with every lotion, medication and bandage I could find. I also bought emergency supplies of baked beans, Vegemite and Milo. If nothing else, I thought, we'd have Dettol and a taste of home.

CHAPTER 3

THE BIG GULP

The sound of the tyres thudding on tarmac sent my mind careering.

The eleven-hour flight with a non-sleeping one-year-old and a three-year-old who really could only take so much colouring-in was finally over. But I wasn't sure we were really ready to get off the plane. I also wasn't convinced tracksuits bought on special at Gold Coast end-of-season sales were going to be warm enough to stand a real Shanghai winter or even protect us for the trip from Pudong International Airport to the city centre.

Exhausted, clutching children, toys and wearing so many layers of clothing we had to walk sideways down the aircraft aisle, I wondered fleetingly if we should just hide on the plane in the hope it turned around and took us home. But that would be crazy.

And so we arrived.

Approaching Shanghai in the taxi from the airport was like entering a giant amusement park still under construction. Gaily painted blue and orange heavy-duty trucks loaded with rubble, cement pipes, giant logs and, in some cases, whole trees with branches hanging out the sides, hogged the highways. Cranes rose disconcertingly regularly from the yellow haze. The honking of horns created a merry kind of cacophony and there was a haphazard adherence to lane markings which gave a white-knuckle sense of excitement to the journey, if you avoided looking at just how often the traffic resulted in devastating pile-ups. We were an hour out of town, it was about 10.30 p.m. on a Thursday and it was like rush hour.

'There must be a really big fire here,' said Milly, staring wide-eyed at this strange new place we'd brought her. 'Look at all that smoke.'

It wasn't smoke, it was smog. And we could see it settling over the city like a circus tent. 'Isn't it great,' we tried to enthuse, already practising shallow breathing in the vain hope that would somehow protect our lungs. The city wasn't only noisy, it was dirty and full of glass and concrete grey, but it had the look of promise. There was neon and activity. And as we held on to our seats, we grinned at each other like fools.

Pudong literally means east of the river. It is the area east of the Huangpu River that, until 1990, was undeveloped farmland and vastly different to Shanghai's city hub on the west of the river called Puxi. Pudong International Airport opened in 1999 in what is

officially called Pudong New Area. In 1990, farmers were told they
had to make way for progress. Now, where there was flat land criss-
crossed by vegetables patches and crop fields, there is the Luijiazui
Finance and Trade Zone. The Pudong skyline is fast becoming the
most recognisable vision of Shanghai, rivalling the famous Bund that
stretches along the Huangpu bank cross river. The Bund may feature
an astounding array of architectural styles among the buildings that
housed the headquarters of the famous trading houses and be the
historical focal point of the city, but Pudong shows off with the
dazzling Oriental Pearl Tower, Jin Mao Building and Shanghai World
Financial Centre, China's tallest building until the 632-metre twisting
skyscraper of the Shanghai Tower is built beside it.

Pudong profoundly illustrates Shanghai's drive for modernisation
and is used by the government as a symbol of China's reform and
opening up. It has about 1.5 million residents, many of whom have
been attracted to the district from Puxi, other parts of China, and
increasingly from overseas to bolster its commercial and financial
stocks. It features mainly finance, high-tech and logistics firms and
accounts for about one quarter of Shanghai's total gross domestic
product.

But at nearly midnight and with two dreadfully weary children,
the bright lights of Pudong, and for that matter Puxi, were going to
have to wait. We were shown an apartment in the continentally-
named La Residence tower on Zhenning Road at the edge of the
French Concession that we had been invited to stay in until we
could find our own digs. Our jovial Australian host Bernie Leo said
he had rustled up a few things to help us settle in. On the stove, he
showed us a blackened frying pan. On the fridge there was a large

bottle of water to be used for drinking and cooking. He told us not to touch the tap water. Rather than being safe to drink even after boiling, it was actually the amount of chemicals in the water killing the bugs that made it unsafe, he said. I was worried about Nelson who still had a habit of drinking bath water. Bernie told me when his two-year-old grandson came to visit, they bathed him in bottled water every day because he had the same tendency. Bernie also pointed out some mini mandarins in the fridge and eggs with a picture of a chicken on the pack. And on the table he proudly showed us bread and a bottle of Vegemite he'd bought in Shanghai. It's not easy finding bread that tastes like bread, he said.

It was late Thursday and we were facing our new reality in China. In three days, Smarty would be starting work on Monday, January 6, at the *Shanghai Daily*, the largest English-only language daily in the city. I would have two weeks to get our life in order before I too started at the paper full-time. At least we had bread.

It's always cold in Shanghai in January. But this year, Bernie told us, it was worse than usual. We woke dehydrated from having the heating turned up too high in the apartment to prevent the shivering. It was our first day. We decided it was time to go outdoors.

Wearing all of the clothes from our suitcase – I packed most of our thick winter gear in the boxes that set sail from Queensland in late October to make way in our luggage for Smarty's office attire – we ventured out of La Residence hoping to find somewhere for the children to play and, perhaps, some good Chinese food.

Shanghai cold isn't like ski-fields cold, or even Canberra cold. It's damp, it's through to the bone and it bites. It even looks miserable.

Nelson, who had spent a significant portion of his young life running around nude, took some convincing to even wear a jacket. We had no hope with a hat. Within a minute of leaving the building we made a checklist to buy a few extra things. We needed mittens or gloves, and scarves, and boots and thick socks and more clothes, and hats that would be impossible for even the grumpiest toddler to remove. And something that smelled really nice. For the smell right outside was dreadful.

Zhenning Road, or Zhenning Lu in local parlance, was actually a terrific street. Cyclists wrapped in scarves and facemasks did battle with motorbike riders who had special fleece-lined handwarmers attached to their handlebars, and taxis and cars and vans and the occasional truck. Every traffic light change seemed to compound staggering traffic jams. Tall residential apartment compounds rose from each side of the street interspersed with barber shops, massage parlours, tailors and convenience stores. Outside the convenience store immediately across the street, a man had a cart on which he had balanced mandarins in a pile so high I couldn't bear to let the kids close in case they caused his efforts to roll away. There were alleys that wound their way back from the street frontage. There were people, there was movement and there was noise. As the street stretched away towards the river, it got busier with street food stalls selling steamed and fried dumplings, pizza-slice-sized pieces of scallion pancakes and the local breakfast of *ji dan bing*, sort of a crepe with egg, sauce, coriander and a few mystery ingredients for added crunch. There were knick-knack shops stocked with mops and steel wool and plastic toys. In the opposite direction it was more sedate but led to the French Concession and Huashan Lu and

Changle Lu, two of the more colourful and interesting streets of the city. But as we stood bewildered at the front of our apartment block, the most obvious thing was that it smelled.

Milly refused to walk down the street. So, on top of my backpack, nappy bags, snack bags, and bottles of water slung over my shoulder, I had to hoist my thermal-wearing little bundle of jumpers onto my hip while she buried her nose in her fuzzy pink overcoat and moaned. Smarty had to do the same with Nelson, while trying to push the now-empty pram with one hand. With our heads down as we struggled with the unfamiliar weight of clothing and children and braced against the cold and sour-smelling aroma, Zhenning Lu failed to reveal all its points of interest on that first day. Instead, we managed a terrific view of the footpath. This, in its own way for newcomers to Shanghai, proved beneficial.

We soon learned that descriptions of the Chinese habit of spitting are no exaggeration. Both men and women spit and it is revolting. Worse was the number of locals who decided to suck back and spit just as we passed. Avoiding stepping on a fresh lugey in Shanghai is about as difficult as avoiding cane toads around a rainwater tank stand on a Queensland summer's evening. In a nod to decorum, one kind gent actually caught himself mid-spit as he cycled past so as not to dampen our progress. Unfortunately it got caught in the wind and we had to take evasive action. Very quickly, we all joined Milly's moaning.

We pressed on and finally, relatively unscathed, we made it to the corner. We'd been told by the charming girls at the front desk at La Residence that there was nowhere nearby for children to play, but if we insisted on going outside we should make a right at Yan'an Lu and head towards the Jing'an Temple. Or that was what we thought was the outcome of our great flurry of arm waving, miming and confused looks. We had planned to equip ourselves with a few Mandarin phrases on the plane on the flight over, but the children refused to sleep. And the girls at the front desk of La Residence barely spoke a word of English.

At the intersection of Zhenning Lu and Yan'an Lu, we waited as we worked out how to cross the nine lanes of endless traffic. Locals converged from all around. They beamed at us as the kids snuggled in closer. They chatted in Chinese as our teeth chattered. Women kindly patted the children and made what I assumed to be peace signs, before I realised that in this nation with a strict one-child policy, they were actually congratulating us on having two children. Then their looks of interest turned to concern. Nelson was not wearing a hat. They pulled at the kids' clothes to ensure there was no skin exposed on their little legs and backs. Some even pulled up Milly's jacket to point out that her four layers of clothing were inadequate. We missed two attempts to cross the road – partly as the traffic didn't appear to ever stop, despite red traffic lights and signs of little green walking men on the pedestrian crossings, and partly due to the number of people who had gathered and appeared to grow increasingly aghast at our under-wrapped children.

Dressing appropriately attracts great importance in China and there is really no excuse for failing to do so. Published weather forecasts are accompanied by reminders on how to dress. In papers such as the *Shanghai Daily* it is common to read helpful suggestions in weather reports, even in the summer months, like: 'As the relative humidity in the air is high, people may feel rather bleak. The bureau reminds people to take on more clothes and take an umbrella when going out.' For those who forgot to take their umbrella, the Shanghai Metro began loaning umbrellas to its millions of passengers for free on rainy days. In the trial phase of the program, 70 per cent of people returned the borrowed umbrellas within one week.

It's not only the people who dress to deal with the weather. In winter, even the trees, including the pruned-back plane trees that are such a feature along streets throughout the French Concession, are snuggled inside bound rope jackets, while shrubs are also wrapped up in bamboo matting with a tie around their waist giving them an enviable hourglass figure.

Along Yan'an Lu, as we finally managed to cross the street, the traffic buzzed by. The noise was new to us and the whistle of wind made conversing difficult. It also made it nearly impossible to hear the motorbikes and bicycles that were driven along the footpath until we were beeped from behind to make way for this seeming extra lane of traffic. Our mouths became dry from apologising so much for actually walking on the sidewalk. Amid all the traffic, though, there were surprising splashes of green. As Yan'an Lu forked into the very top of Nanjing Lu, there was a frozen little communal open area where we first saw the winter floral plantings. In the gardens were what appeared to be purple lettuce and cauliflower. They were hardy and covered in frost and we subsequently saw them everywhere. We didn't know whether they were there for aesthetic or practical purposes, but they added a pleasant mauve tint to the city.

It was further down Yan'an Lu that we finally found a park. Parks, or green spaces in town planning jargon, were the buzz in Shanghai as the city geared up for the 2010 World Expo. By the end of 2007, the amount of green space in the city equated to 12 square metres per capita. By 2010, planners projected every resident within the outer ring road (that's about 9.7 million people living in a 670-square kilometre area) would have access to 5000 square metres of green within 500 metres of their home.

Chinese gardens are not just open spaces but constructs of nature designed to showcase the balance of elements and provide a harmonious escape from the harried streets outside. When we stumbled on Jing'an Park, we just saw a big patch of grass. Entering the park was like letting dogs off a leash. Shrugging off our feelings of being stifled under layers of clothes or being stuck inside in the heating, we gambolled about on the grass then the kids rushed off to play hide and seek. Smarty and I moved back to the pathway to let them cut loose for a few minutes. But their freedom was only brief. Soon, park security descended on us. Of course, we had failed to understand the signs warning us not to walk on the grass. Milly decided the waving security official was keen to play hide and seek, and the more the security official chased, the further on to the protected grass she ran, hiding behind perfectly shaped shrubs and strategically placed rock formations. We couldn't help but laugh as the security guard also tried in vain to convince Nelson to get off the grass and they had a face-off, each obviously trying to decide who was more bizarre – the little blond boy in an oversized tracksuit playing on the frozen grass and asking for the slippery-slide, or the gruff looking man trying to explain in Chinese why parks weren't for playing.

Next to the grassy patch, the southern end of Jing'An Park is dominated by a lake and surrounding southern Chinese garden that provides a slice of serenity just metres from busy Yan'an Lu. Miscreants recaptured, we made our way through the rocky garden and past clusters of elderly folk playing mah-jong and others practising Tai Chi. The central avenue of the park had been turned into a makeshift ballroom dancing hall as couples danced along the paved strip to the music of duelling ballroom boom boxes that had been set up on park benches or in baby prams. Where the pathway forked, was where still others had gathered to sing Chinese opera, while a few old men entertained a crowd by writing in classic Chinese calligraphy on the cement. We made our way through and found a small playground. But we didn't last there long. I worried the children's hands would freeze to the iron bars or stick to the edge of the slide, and we seemed to be upsetting the only other person in the incredibly clean park – a man whose job it was to pick up the leaves. He was on to each one in a flash as it fell from the tree and was not amused when the kids grabbed some leaves from the garden to throw at each other.

We made our exit as he busied himself with the leafy litter. It was time to eat. We had been in China less than 24 hours. We had been overwhelmed by our new home, had utterly failed at our first interactions with locals, and struggled to even cross the street. We sought a retreat, but summoned our strength to treat our kids to one more 'first-time experience' which we would not have considered were we back in Australia. And we dived into a McDonald's.

CHAPTER 4

EARLY SETTLERS

There are about 68 000 expats living in Shanghai and almost 19 million Chinese. I was on the phone with one increasingly frustrated Chinese man who was trying to instruct me how to connect my computer to the Internet. The only word I could understand was 'Internet' and I was almost in tears I was so desperate after a week in China to resume e-contact with friends and family in Australia.

My Chinese Internet guy hung up. Somehow, about an hour later a man from China Telecom surprised me by turning up at my door. He also spoke no English. It's remarkable how, when faced with the inability to communicate in a designated foreign tongue, I found myself remembering phrases in various other languages from studies and travels that were equally as useless in the circumstances as English. Though it took about 90 minutes and a lot of puzzling exchanges, we managed to get my laptop online and communicate a log-in and password for subsequent connections – I think.

The reality of living in a country where I didn't even have the most basic grasp of the local language was proving more difficult than I expected. I realised I was suffering from that underlying arrogance many Anglophones share of always assuming English will suffice. And that we probably should have prepared ourselves more rigorously before bringing the family to live in China.

But we were learning. It took a few days, but we decided we could no longer survive on mandarins, noodles-in-a-cup and hamburgers (unlike in Australia, there were no 'healthy options' at McDonald's in China). We figured we would take on local restaurants by degree and start with guide book recommendations for establishments that offered menus with at least a smattering of English. We settled on 1221, a restaurant that offered authentic Shanghai food and which was said to have a following among both foreigners and locals. Their drunken chicken, lionhead meatballs, crispy duck and *la la ji ding*, or spicy cold chicken noodles, sounded tempting. However, the restaurant, named for where it sits at number 1221 Yan'an Lu, was not as close to Zhenning Lu as we anticipated, and as we were walking we fell into step behind a Chinese family with a child about Milly's age. Like us, they were eating early and were heading out to dinner. They stopped about one block before our intended destination at a lively restaurant with a red flashing neon crab at the front and a bunch of eager-looking local diners milling about the entrance. At the sight of a queue, we cast our well-laid 1221 plans aside and decided instead that the flashy crab on Yan'an Lu was the restaurant for us. The restaurant had no English name or menu and, as we were whisked inside, we passed tanks of crabs and fish and tables with steaming black woks inserted into the centre. It smelled captivating. It looked daunting.

We were ushered through the restaurant to a smaller dining room at the back where we were shown to a wok-less table and shared the space with a Chinese couple who were tucking into chicken feet and something black and slippery. The menu we were presented with had no English, but it did have pictures. Charged with the task of ordering for the family, I began eliminating. Chicken feet were out, as were all manner of gizzards and eel. I couldn't quite discern from the pictures what was contained in each dish and, panic rising, looked over at our fellow diners to see if they had ordered anything that looked palatable or child-friendly so we could choose the same meal. Alas, they were still picking at their chicken feet. I was poised to order. I pointed to my first choice of dish and inquiringly made clucking noises to check that it was indeed chicken. The waitress responded with a shake of her head and a croak. I signalled a negative on the bullfrog. I ordered three dishes. I was pretty sure one had prawns.

While we were waiting for our dinner, Milly informed us she would no longer eat Chinese food. It was because she was Australian. She would, therefore, only eat Australian food. We asked which Australian food, precisely, she planned to sustain herself with. 'Only spaghetti,' she said. 'And sometimes pizza.' Perhaps we had chosen the wrong country. Nelson, on the other hand, was loving it. There were cars and trucks everywhere. And he'd eat anything.

Our food arrived. One dish did contain prawns, with great clumps of sizzling garlic. It was delicious and both children jumped at the food. I caught Milly hungrily devouring the prawns, complete with shells and heads. Another dish had rice and Nelson claimed it as his own, while the third was a mystery. We picked at the tender meat and the bones in the brown sauce. It wasn't the crab I expected. It wasn't fish. It was slightly sweet while the sauce disguised whether it was a red meat or chicken. It was very enjoyable and I lapped up the congratulations on ordering our first English-free Chinese meal. And then, at the bottom of the bowl, we found a head. It would appear the mystery third dish was duck.

We decided to grab a taxi on the way back to La Residence. There are about 45 000 taxis in Shanghai. If it is raining, that's not enough. Otherwise, they are generally plentiful and easy to hail and are usually very clean with a white cover on the rear seat. Drivers are fined if there are dirty marks on the seat and can get very cross if children clamber in without showing due care. Taxis are also very cheap. The cost is 11 yuan (about A$1.80) for the first three kilometres, or 14 yuan if travelling late at night. After that every kilometre costs about 2 yuan (about A$0.30). Taxi drivers must display their experience level on the cab dashboard. They all show a taxi licence, with a photograph, which includes a six digit number. The lower the number, the longer the taxi driver has been on the road as the licences are issued sequentially. A star ranking usually sits below the number. New drivers get no stars while drivers with more than three years' experience get two stars. Three stars apparently mean the driver has been in the business a while and won't get lost. In my limited early dealings with Chinese locals, I found it was taxi drivers who were most likely to have a little English. The two I had managed to speak with had both had the same response to that international ice-breaker: 'Where are you from?' It was delivered with a big thumbs-up. 'Ah, Odaliya (Australia). Kangaroo, koala, Kevin Rudd.' In the K-cubed response, it was the former Prime Minister's ability to speak Mandarin they were most impressed with.

There are no seat belts in Shanghai's taxis and the drivers zip through traffic at breakneck speeds. Yet it was fun to catch cabs in the city if only to read the English translation of the taxi rules. The lack of political correctness matched only the lack of safety precautions, with the sign claiming drivers could evict 'alcoholics' or 'retardeds' who are unaccompanied. We tried not to laugh too much. We weren't yet beyond '*nihao*' (hello) in Chinese.

As we were so new to Shanghai, and taxis were so cheap, we didn't even consider buses or the Metro to get around. After Smarty headed off to work, I decided I'd had enough of stressing about getting our life together. The Shanghai Zoo didn't look that far away from our apartment on the map, so I bundled the kids in a cab and pointed the driver at a picture of a panda in a cage in the hope he would take us to the zoo.

There are very few people in Shanghai who would choose to visit the zoo in early January. The icy wind whistled around the deserted entrance area as the kids and I fought our way against the sleet to get to the ticket booth. There was no wait. We got straight in. On entering the zoo, there was a long avenue lined with the winter skeletons of plane trees and frozen grass. It looked far more delightful in the brochures where it was advertised as one of the biggest grassy spaces in the city and was packed with happy visitors and Chinese people flying kites, playing games and practising Tai Chi. We walked the barren path to the lizard exhibit where I consulted the map and realised that the animals we had come to see – lions, tigers and pandas – were all at the far end of the zoo grounds. With the children already asking me to carry them and complaining about the cold, I didn't think I was going to be able to cope. Then I spied the zoo train. We were the only three on the train and, feeling a little like royalty, we were whisked around on a private tour of the zoo. We tried to visit the lions and tigers first, but it was so cold the animals were all huddled, unmoving, in a corner of their enclosures. It was on to the pandas. I was as excited as the kids as we rushed to the inside viewing area to see the cuddly-looking creatures that are the symbol and pride of China. Visiting the pandas in the zoo in winter, however, is frankly not a sight I'd recommend. On our visit there were three pandas. Each was in its own glass-fronted enclosure. All were sitting on a cold concrete floor with a few pieces of bamboo strewn around. Two weren't moving. One was clearly agitated and started doing lap after lap of his tiny pen, bashing himself with greater intensity into the glass on each pass. A few other visitors were pressed up against the glass taking photographs and laughing. I just felt sad, but reasoned the animals were perhaps only in this state because it was winter and the dank pen was preferable to being outside in the cold. The children didn't like the view either, so we jumped back aboard the train and asked to return to our starting point. We all felt so deflated I agreed to take the kids on the ferris wheel ride near the flamingo pond.

Safety standards in China don't appear quite as stringent as we're accustomed to in Australia. The comparison occurred to me as the zoo ferris wheel stopped with us perched at its highest point. We were caught in the crosswind, which caused the capsule to swing and sway. The structure holding us up started clunking and groaning. It was so old it looked like it was made entirely of wood. Of course we were the only ones aboard. I did my best not to show the kids my raw fear. I couldn't think why I considered what looked like an antiquated death trap at the Shanghai Zoo a good idea for the kids' first ferris wheel ride. We signalled to get off after one rotation and clambered back aboard the zoo train. At the entry gate the driver helped me off and slugged me 400 yuan (A$65) for the trip. I was so shaken by the ferris wheel, upset about the pandas, worried about the kids, and still plain confused about the exchange rate that I didn't even realise I'd been ripped off terribly until we were back out of the gate and in a taxi on the way home.

In the taxi I realised I'd forgotten the card with directions to La Residence. My frozen lips wouldn't let me pronounce Zhenning Lu (the Zh has a sound like tse, as in tsetse fly). I kept trying. On about the fiftieth attempt, the taxi driver thumped the steering wheel and started laughing. He then said Zhenning Lu in a manner that sounded to me exactly like I'd been saying the past twenty times. When we pulled up at La Residence he was still chuckling. After our big day out I failed to see the humour.

It was the language barrier that really had me fretting. I had to find somewhere for the family to live and someone to care for the children before I started work. Thankfully, Ted Howse, another 'foreign expert' from the Shanghai Daily, put me in touch with a Chinese real estate agent. I'd decided to forego any more sightseeing trips and call her straight away. Yuki spoke English very well. I was so relieved, I found myself babbling to her about everything from the weather to the differences between the football codes played in Australia. We had decided we would like to live in Shanghai's former French Concession, and had romantic notions of finding a house in one of the fascinating *longtang* (residential lanes) which were once emblematic of the city, but are quickly disappearing along with Shanghai's classic *shikumen* (stone-gated) houses.

There is probably no area in Shanghai more famous than the former French Concession. It's where *haipai*, the meld of Chinese tradition and Western modernity, or Shanghai style, was born. In depictions of Shanghai as the 'Paris of the East', the French Concession is always the focus. Rows of mottled plane trees or sycamores, known in China as French planes, distinguish its avenues from the colder glass and steel streetscapes of many other districts. There are cosmopolitan galleries, boutiques, restaurants, cafés and nightspots opening onto the streets and tucked away in alleys. Diplomatic quarters are dotted throughout the area and some of the city's most stylish and renowned residences are on display. The French Concession has long been known for attracting artists, intellectuals and adventurers and has a reputation for not only being stylish by day, but quite naughty by night. It is also the area in which some of China's most prominent characters have preferred to live. Chinese revolutionary leader and founder of the Kuomintang, Dr Sun Yat-sen, lived and received members of the Communist Party of China at his two-storey home on Xiangshan Lu. After Sun's death, his wife, Madame Soong Ching Ling, remained based in the French Concession at 1843 Huaihai Lu. The first Premier of the People's

Republic of China, Zhou Enlai, acclaimed novelist Ba Jin and Peking Opera master Mei Lanfang all also lived in the French Concession, as did composer Nie Er who created 'March of the Volunteers', which became China's national anthem, in his Huaihai Lu apartment.

Middle Huaihai Lu, formerly known as Avenue Joffre, is the epicentre of the French Concession and still bears traces indicating why it was dubbed the 'Champs-Elysees of the Orient'. In the 1920s, it was said the latest Paris trends would appear on stylish Avenue Joffre within one week. I found it lovely to look at the latest fashions still on offer along the street, though I had no hope of fitting into anything in the Chinese boutiques. I could, however, picture myself window shopping frequently if I were to make the strip my neighbourhood.

Buzzing with the idea of finding a nook in the beautiful and historical French Concession that we could call our home, I told Yuki that I didn't know what style of accommodation to seek and was prepared to consider anything we could afford from lane houses to *lilong*, which are rather basic residential compounds built by foreigners for Chinese residents during the mid 1800s. Yuki, however, suggested we might be more comfortable in a modern apartment complex. I was running out of time to find somewhere. I took the kids and went where I was told.

Jing'an is not quite the French Concession. But it has the oldest shrine in the city, the Jing'an Temple, that dates back to 247 AD. The Buddhist temple predates the city of Shanghai itself and its name means 'peace and tranquillity'. The stunning wooden and golden pagoda structure is located on bustling Nanjing Lu next to a ritzy shopping strip and across from a Metro station. It is hardly the most serene locale.

Jing'an also has a plethora of modern apartment compounds. Smarty and I each had a monthly accommodation allowance of 7500 yuan (A$1220.64). Yuki took me to about 12 different apartments in our price range. I knew we'd secured a very generous housing allowance, but I was still unprepared for the options I was presented with for our new home. As we pushed open the doors to each new apartment, the children looked at me inquiringly. They'd come from a house with stairs and levels, a bedroom each, a yard to play in, and a dog. The apartments we saw were not at all child-friendly and some didn't even have room to keep a fish. Those that did were stuffed with such ornate Chinese-style furniture that I didn't even dare let the kids get to the stage of taking their shoes off so they could enter. At perhaps the ninth apartment we visited, Milly decided she'd had enough of holding back and rushed in to see which room she might claim as her bedroom. She chose one and excitedly attempted to open a large, antique-looking bureau, only to pull the drawer handle clean off. I apologised profusely and slunk back out into the cold without submitting a rental application.

Yuki finally told me she thought she had the answer to our needs. She took us all to inspect a three bedroom apartment in the 'One Park Avenue' complex on the corner of Xinzha and Changle roads in Jing'an. One Park is a largely expat compound, but is also home to many wealthier Chinese. It has a club house with an indoor swimming pool, ping-pong tables, karaoke room, gym and squash court. It also has a children's play room and outside it has gardens with pathways and lagoons and two sets of play equipment in the

centre of its ten 34-storey towers. There are about 1300 apartments
in the complex, which takes up less than a city block. I was starting
to understand the concept of Shanghai's high density living. I was
also starting to grasp some of the benefits of apartment living (like a
clubhouse). Although we might be sharing the address with
thousands of other people, One Park Avenue felt like an oasis. It had
outdoor space and grass and the kids begged to burn off some energy
on the playroom see-saws and in the ball pit. They then assessed the
pathways between the towers and declared them perfect for riding
their bikes and the little four-wheeler 'wheely bug' shaped like a
cow that I packed for Nelson along with our baked beans, Milo
and Vegemite.

The apartment was fully furnished. We were in the middle of
Shanghai, yet I felt like I'd just stepped into the Swedish surrounds
of an IKEA catalogue. It was full of indestructible timber furniture
and was light and airy and didn't feel like we were going to have to
tiptoe around the apartment and spend our entire time scolding the
children for damaging antiques. It didn't feel anything like home,
but it was the best option for our family we'd seen. The kids loved
it and staged a sit-in. They could see somewhere to play, somewhere
to swim, and realised they may not have to visit any more
apartments. We were about mid-way up Tower 4 on the 20th floor.
Yuki told me it was a good height as mosquitoes that can spread
dengue fever and Japanese encephalitis usually only fly as high as
level 15. We were just out of harm's way as the building, like many
in superstitious China, didn't have a floor 4, 13 or 14. It seemed
like a good neighbourhood and we enjoyed the view from the
bedroom windows which took in a chaotic intersection and a

city-block-sized building site. I took a good look at all the fittings provided in the apartment and pressed a few buttons by way of making sure it all worked. The writing on all the appliances was in Chinese. I was either going to have to get translations for the washing machine or buy everyone in the family 365 new pairs of underwear.

The apartment didn't fit my romantic notion of living in a historic Chinese lane house or a flat previously occupied by one of the characters from the city's colourful past. Jing'an also didn't come close to the hip, dynamic atmosphere of the French Concession. Apart from the foreign appliance instructions, there was very little about the apartment that showed we were even living in China. It was comfortable, clean, modern and safe, but could be an apartment in any city in the world, if we didn't look out the windows or take in the cooking smells wafting in from neighbouring flats. But we liked it. We were all exhausted from looking at apartments and were desperate to find somewhere to unpack our things. We were tired of feeling like our adventure was on hold and were eager to start our life in Shanghai. Without looking any further, we applied for the apartment. Yuki told us there shouldn't be a problem as long as we could come up with the 45 000-yuan (A$7300) deposit. Smarty and I celebrated no longer being homeless.

While I set about moving from La Residence and making our new apartment a bit homey, Smarty used his time walking to and from work to investigate the neighbourhood. He said he had located a source for cheap, knock-off DVDs. He bought me a copy of the Tom Cruise, Meryl Streep drama, *Lions for Lambs* for which he paid 5 yuan (A$0.80). He said he bought it from a guy on the street because copies in the store near the newspaper office were much more expensive at 12 yuan (A$1.95). Unfortunately, the movie was in Russian. It even contained the coughs and spluttering of the person making the illegal recording. It was hilarious. I couldn't bring myself to watch a legitimate version of the movie – it was unlikely to contain the same number of laughs.

Smarty had been very busy. He had also bought us mobile phones. He brought home the receipts to show me the warranty information handwritten on the back. The instructions stated that 'if you think this mobile has everyone is bread, you must go to No 96 at Middle Fujian Road for repair. In seven days we can help you exit or change new one. In fifteen days we can only help you change new one. If you know please write your name'. We crossed our fingers and hoped the phones would work.

The new apartment was quite close to the newspaper office, yet that didn't stop Smarty looking into buying a bike to get to and from work. While there had been an explosion in private car ownership in China, especially in wealthy Shanghai where the narrow streets were often clogged with the latest model Buicks, SUVs and even Hummers, bicycles remained the preeminent mode of transport around the city. Shanghai may have been spiked with modern skyscrapers, pumping construction sites and monstrous elevated highways, but the Chinese people who built them still relied largely on pedal power to get around.

The China Bicycle Association said there were about 500 million bicycles on China's mainland. There were more than 10 million bikes in Shanghai. I hadn't seen any bike paths. Or a bike helmet. Cyclists sat in the heaviest traffic. Grim-faced and with steely determination, they took on rumbling trucks and buses through gridlocked intersections. At traffic lights, where the concept of lanes disintegrated as drivers pushed to catch the final fraction of a second before a red light, it was bicyclists who triumphantly streamed through the snarls from the green-light cross streets like spilt milk seeping around an obstruction. With cotton masks filtering out exhaust fumes, cyclists wound their way through rush hour traffic, weaving on and off footpaths so their progress was rarely halted. There was every type of bicycle imaginable. Shanghai Forever was China's largest bicycle maker and their old heavy duty standard issue model remained popular. Women in high heels and businessmen in suits made up a large slice of the bicycle commuters, all on their standard bicycles with briefcases and handbags in the basket at the front or on the rear carrier.

There were bikes for children, bikes for the disabled, bikes that folded up until they almost fit into a briefcase. There were bikes for business. Snack bikes pulled up at the corners of busy streets with what looked like 44-gallon drums slung either side of the rear wheel. At the top of the drums were sweet potatoes, slowly roasting on the fire in the barrel beneath. There were bikes carrying chestnuts and fitted with measuring scales, bikes with every sort of vegetable in season and bicycles with freshly killed chickens dangling from the carrier. Bikes with little trailers behind clanged through the city with the riders ringing a small bell. This was the call to bring out any recyclables for collection. Bikes packed with wares were constantly on the move to try to attract customers. On Wuyuan Lu, in the French Concession, I was puzzled by a convoy of bicycles paused for a moment outside a shop that seemed to sell nothing but posters of

Brazilian soccer star Ronaldinho. The bikes all had trays loaded with mops, tea towels, slippers, hangers, socks, hats, gloves, steel wool and novelty toys. I wondered who their target market was.

Bikes were used to transport everything imaginable. We were left gobsmacked by what the Chinese could carry on a two-wheeler. We watched as cyclists pedalled down the street carrying upwards of twenty polystyrene containers, giant flower arrangements, computers, mattresses, even refrigerators. At the intersection of Shaanxi and Nanjing roads one day, we were stunned when a middle-aged man nonchalantly pulled up at the red light carrying on his bike a TV, a computer and a fridge.

It seemed everybody in Shanghai could ride a bike and almost all owned their own bicycle. As recently as the 1970s, the three most valuable assets a Chinese family could own were a bicycle, a sewing machine and a watch. The items were known as 'The Old Three' and were considered generous wedding gifts for young couples. However, since China's reform and opening up from 1978, with its accompanying rise in living standards, 'The Old Three' had been replaced by 'The New Three' in terms of customary wedding gifts. In the 1980s, The New Three meant a TV, a washing machine and a fridge. In the '90s, it meant a colour TV, a car and jewellery. Now, it was anything goes. Young couples usually already both had bicycles.

Smarty said a colleague from work had offered him the use of his bicycle. It was a classic old 'Giant Khan'. He decided to ride it home. Unfortunately, he was too scared to take a corner and ended up many blocks out of his way, swept along in the flow of traffic before he got off and walked back towards our apartment. I asked him to stick, for the time being, to his 20 minute walk to work.

Apart from modes of transport, Smarty had also been battling some of the hurdles thrown up by our Chinese work place. Unsurprisingly, the keyboard commands on his computer were in Chinese. He had been assigned to give advice on the layout and design of the paper and produce the cover story and some inside pages of the newspaper's daily feature section. It was not that easy using Chinese character command keys. He said he had worked out that the command symbol that looked like a man wearing a funny hat would print out a page proof. That wasn't bad for almost two weeks on the job. He had, however, faced even more basic problems. It appeared the toilet cubicles in the office were not designed for gents of a tall-ish stature. He said every time he bent to use the toilet, he hit the cubicle door with either his knees or his forehead. He had become quite embarrassed with all the banging and groaning in pain that accompanied his visits to the bathroom.

Work was looming for me and I felt that in the fortnight since we had arrived, we'd got through a lot of the harder tasks in setting ourselves up in Shanghai. But there was still a lot to get organised in the next few days. I looked from our new apartment window to the bleakness outside. I could sense things were slowly improving. It was no longer quite so grey. It had started snowing.

CHAPTER 5

LESSONS IN RIVALRY

Up shot her eyebrows. I knew what was coming next. I'd already been to four different kindergartens and had received a similar reaction each time.

'We haven't actually been asked that before,' the principal said. 'What you want is quite unusual and no, we don't do that at all. Three-year-olds in China go to kindergarten the whole week and the whole day.'

With a couple of weeks in Shanghai under our belts we'd started to regain a sense of control. I'd found somewhere for us to live, Smarty was happily heading off to work, we had food to eat at night. Now I needed to concentrate on the kids. They were getting heartily sick of being cooped up inside or rugging up to head out into the cold for something as boring as shopping for pots and pans. So I tried to find Milly a Shanghai kindergarten to attend. I wanted her to have the experience of kindergarten but didn't want her there every day, or even for too long on the days she did attend. I was going to be working full-time from 5.00 p.m. to 1.00 a.m., which meant I would get to see very little of her if she was constantly at kindy. Plus, I had to work Sundays, giving me one day off during the week, and I wanted to spend it with both kids having fun in Shanghai. So I was looking for a flexible arrangement – and one which I had expected would be quite commonplace given my limited experience with child-care and kindergartens for three-year-olds in Australia.

But every kindy I tried rigidly offered only 9.00 a.m. to 4.00 p.m. five days a week. That was longer than school hours. There was no option for three days a week , or to go home with Mum at lunchtime. Puzzled by my request, most principals said attending only for half-days meant the child would miss out on afternoon lessons.

That most three-year-olds in Shanghai were busy doing lessons all day, every day did explain why we were finding it hard to track down other children to play with. I'd been expecting to rely on the universally accepted method of befriending other parents by allowing the kids to meet other children in the sandpit or playground, become 'best friends' within minutes, and then offer to meet up again for an arranged playdate. But I had drawn a miserable blank in Shanghai. Now I was beginning to understand. It wasn't just that no-one else was crazy enough to take their children outside to play in the depths of a freezing winter. The children were all in school.

There are about 1000 kindergartens in Shanghai taking care of more than 300 000 children. Our arrival coincided with a boom in kindergarten construction, with the local political advisory body suggesting another 500 kindergartens were needed to cope with demand in Shanghai. The reason was that despite the one-child policy, there had been an explosion in the number of babies being born. The surge in births was largely due to the Chinese belief that babies born in the lunar Chinese year of the pig – 2007 and early 2008 – are lucky. The year 2007 was the year of the 'Golden Pig' which occurs every 60 years and is the luckiest time to have a baby. Figures presented to the Shanghai Municipal Committee of the Chinese People's Political Consultative Conference in January 2008 showed more than 160 000 babies were born in Shanghai in 2007, up 20 per cent on the previous year. It said as many as 170 000 newborns were expected in 2008 when people were also trying for an 'Olympic baby'.

It was not just regular kindergartens springing up in Shanghai. Boarding schools for kindergarten-aged children had been growing in popularity. The *Shanghai Daily* reported that there were 100 boarding schools from kindergarten to high school grades in the city. On average it cost 2500 yuan (A$407) a month to board a child at a primary school in the city, compared with 170 yuan (A$27) at a non-boarding one. At some high schools, room and board could cost 5000 yuan (A$815). Kindergarten boarders, many as young as two, were generally of middle and upper-class parents who made the financial sacrifice as they were so keen for their children to get ahead. The parents were also usually so busy working themselves that boarding kindergartens were considered a good childcare option.

In Shanghai, general local kindergartens are ranked in four levels – campus, level one, two and three – according to criteria such as facilities, faculty and hygiene. Most campus schools, the top level, provide a bilingual education and foreign teachers. There are also many private kindergartens that offer bi-lingual education and target largely expat children. I thought one of these kindergartens would be the best option for Milly, but the cost was a shock with most asking upwards of 50 000 yuan (A$8150) a year in fees. One kindergarten I approached to ask about programs for Milly charged 92 000 yuan (A$14 997) a year for three-year-olds. The fees compared to about A$30 000 to $50 000 a year for primary and high schools. Many expats in Shanghai who sent their children to these schools were on packages where tuition was covered by their employer. More and more expats though, especially those losing elements of their package in the belt-tightening environment of the global financial crisis, were having to look to local schools and kindergartens.

There was immense competition to get into local kindergartens. The right kindergarten and the right results could help a child win a place in a good primary school. We had arrived in Shanghai as the season for admissions to city primary schools was hitting top gear. Dong Lei, the mother of a five-year-old girl, told the *Shanghai Daily* she and other parents had been putting together résumés to submit to primary schools in the hope their children gained entry. She admitted it sounded terrible putting the sort of pressures on little children that adults face when seeking employment. But, she said, everyone was doing it so those who didn't got left behind. Standard résumés included basic information – name, nickname, height, weight, personality and a picture – as well as the toddler's other academic and extracurricular experience. In China there are any number of formal piano lessons, violin, ballet and martial arts training programs for tots. These achievements, along with Chinese and English language proficiency, were included in the baby CVs along with examples of the child's writing and artwork. I was quite horrified by the competitiveness and the effect it must have on children and decided to leave my kids' squiggly finger paintings on the fridge, where they belonged.

Trying to find the right kindergarten for Milly proved anything but simple. I tried explaining to the principals that I was really only looking to send her so she could continue the one-day-a-week introduction she had to kindergarten in Australia and meet some new friends. I expected to be a bit weary from working full-time on evening shifts and it was awful weather for playing outside, so I was looking to enrol her to help keep her stimulated and engaged in fun activities I didn't feel I could offer at home every day. I was sure she'd cope with being in a brand new environment with no friends, unfamiliar teachers, a different language to most of her classmates and having to eat the snacks and lunches provided by the kindergarten, though she was still in her phase of refusing Chinese food. But I was not happy about the rigidity of kindy curriculums I was being shown where the day was broken into lessons of Chinese, English and maths with extra classes in computers, music and physical exercise.

The enrolment officer at Happy Marian kindergarten on Changle Lu near Fumin Lu seemed to take pity on me. 'We do have half-day programs,' she said. 'But they are only for babies. And that's still five days a week.' In China, the kindy babies are one-year-olds, not my little three-year-old. I hadn't even considered sending one-year-old Nelson to kindergarten. Would he have to do lessons too? The principal said she could make an exception for Milly. She said she was prepared to let us pay for a full-time enrolment, but only attend part-time.

After saying no, I walked away baffled. It seemed to be the prevailing belief in China that it was vital to start children in formal education as early as possible. The experience of talking to the kindergarten principals made me feel as if, by keeping my kids at home, I was stunting their academic growth by letting them play with playdough and papier-mâché while their counterparts in China were at kindergarten all day reading, writing and developing their brains at a rate of knots. Being in a foreign country where accepted practices and norms are not only unfamiliar but challenge what we think is best for our kids was testing. I was even more thrown because the kindergartens where the principals were so surprised I didn't want Milly attending full-time, or Nelson attending at all, catered for expat children as well as Chinese kids. I was taken aback that so many expat children in China were also attending kindergartens and starting on full-time formal curriculums by the age of three.

In Australia much of the thinking on early childhood education had been focused on play-based learning. Three-year-olds staying at home playing with sticks, watching clouds and having naps was actually considered okay. My understanding had been that under-fives who went to kindergartens, preschools and childminding centres in Australia were not put in strictly timed classes for teacher-led lessons, but rather were invited to join an activity or generally allowed to pursue a game, craft or subject that had piqued their interest. The education debates that had cropped up seemed to concentrate instead on whether to push back the age at which children started compulsory schooling and the age at which they finished.

In the months before leaving for China, we saw that Queensland was wrapping up a trial year of Prep, effectively giving children in the state an extra year of the school experience but starting them in Grade 1 at a slightly older age. The change aimed to bring Queensland in line with most of the other Australian states that offered a Prep year, although the age cut-off (which in Queensland required a child to turn five before July 1 in the year they start Prep) still differed between states. The Prep introduction was backed by experts telling us that children were more likely to thrive on starting the formal school system from Grade 1 later rather than earlier. Simultaneously, I saw the United States was reporting a trend of an increasing number of children delaying or repeating preschool or their first year of schooling so they would get an advantage in the system by being older and, hopefully, more mature and able. The push for children to start school at a later age was also gaining force in the United Kingdom. The Cambridge Primary Review, a major ongoing enquiry into the condition and future of primary education in England, suggested in an interim report that an early start to education offered kids no long-term advantages. It said a later starting age in the UK would also bring a uniformity to schooling in the European Union where many countries, including Sweden, Denmark and Finland, already had a starting age for compulsory schooling of seven years.

But in Shanghai, it appeared to me nobody was looking to start their child in the education system later. The kindergarten principals I spoke to even told me parents often asked for an earlier age at which their child could start and longer hours because both parents had to work.

I dragged the kids in the icy weather to at least ten kindergartens. Finally, we found one that seemed to offer some flexibility and was affordable. It was right across the road from La Residence, the apartment block we stayed in when we first arrived. The kindergarten was called Mother Goose, a Singapore-based organisation. The principal, Mrs Teh, agreed to Milly starting on a basis of three half-days a week until she got settled. The brightly decorated rooms of the kindergarten seemed cosy and clean and there was a mixture of expat and Chinese children inside who were playing, with some dancing around to music. There was no shortage of teachers – an English language speaker, a Mandarin speaker and at least one extra helper for each of the four classes. It offered some play-based learning, though set out a full curriculum in subjects including Chinese language, English language, maths and computing. Milly spied some of the toys and the other children and said she was keen to give it a try, starting straight away. I was thrilled, but still wary. The process had me exhausted.

I told my kindy caper story at dinner with friends Jane, a Shanghai local, and her Swedish husband, Thomas, whom we met in One Park Avenue. Their four-year-old daughter also attended Mother Goose. They agreed the Chinese system could be extremely rigorous and we compared the more relaxed Australian and Swedish education experience. I'm not convinced Australia has the system right for our kids, but I couldn't agree, even from the little I'd learned, that China had either. There was another Chinese couple at dinner. Their son had been slumped in his chair most of the night, only looking up when he was spoken to directly, at which time he would offer a quick answer, with a display of perfect manners, before crumbling back into his wilted state.

His father explained that though his son was only fourteen, he had been at school for about nine hours that day. It was a Saturday. He had been up since 5.30 a.m. every day, at school from 8 a.m. to 5 p.m., returning home for dinner before hitting the books again for homework until about 10 p.m. He had weekend lessons, so had no time to play. The boy was simply worn out. His parents were worried for him, but said they couldn't change the system. If he didn't do the work and put in the extreme hours, they told us, other children would and would get ahead while their son was left behind. They all had no choice. But that didn't mean they liked it.

The boy's father said he feared the workload was turning out students anxious and drained of enjoyment while the devotion to rote learning was killing creativity among Chinese youth. 'We can learn what has already been discovered and put it into practice better than anyone else, but how many Chinese have won a Nobel Prize?' he said. 'No-one these days can stop and think or create.'

There have been seven Nobel laureates born or raised in Chinese territory or had Chinese roots, including 2000 Nobel Literature laureate Gao Xingjian, whose work has been banned in China since 1986 and who has been living in exile since 1987. But it is a big deal in China that no Chinese national has ever won a Nobel Prize and that the Chinese Communist government cannot claim one of its own citizens – born, educated and living within the system – as winner of the prestigious award.

It was not only over dinner tables and in lounge rooms that concerns were being aired over the early start to school and immense pressure Chinese school students are under. The pressure for academic achievement started at toddler age. At Chinese kindergartens, children had their study schedule tightened and nap time reduced from about May in readiness for the start of primary school in September. The kindy kids got one more lesson added to their daily schedule to reduce the 'shock' they may experience starting school. Primary school right from Grade 1 was much more intense and very exam oriented.

Columnist Wan Lixin wrote in the *Shanghai Daily* that academic success, even at that young age, has a profound impact on the rest of a child's life. 'The "good" students, or those good at getting high scores, are pampered and fawned over by the teachers and the students alike, in spite of their defects in other respects. The "bad" students are perennial victims of prejudice, disdain, and neglect,' he said. Wan Lixin said school cramming is institutionalised and compulsory. He said many students end up traumatised, but individual resistance can be futile. 'My five-year-old son is attending a kindergarten known for its English teaching, but so far we have managed to show little concern over his ignorance compared with his classmates,' he said. 'But our protection can go only as far as elementary school, where he will be constantly ranked in accordance with his score, which then dictates the amount of respect and kindness he will get from his teachers and classmates.'

The director of the Institute of Youth and Juveniles with the Shanghai Academy of Social Sciences, Professor Yang Xiong, told the newspaper that parents are placing excessive expectations on their children. He said while Chinese kids today are more knowledgeable than in the past, they are facing new problems not only limited to a lack of sleep and free time. They are suffering anxiety over their performance and, with their every waking moment focused on academic pursuits, are even suffering in skills for daily life. 'It's sad that some primary school students still don't know how to tie their shoes or take a bath on their own,' he said.

Highlighting this pressure on China's children, the *Shanghai Daily* covered the tragic story of a thirteen-year-old boy who committed suicide as he could no longer handle the pressure of school. Another columnist at the newspaper, Wu Jiayin, said such terrible stories are not isolated incidents, especially around September when the new school year begins. He reported that a day earlier a fourteen-year-old girl jumped from her fourth-floor apartment in Shanghai's Yangpu District. She faced losing her eyesight. The same day, a fifteen-year-old boy in Pudong 'fell' from his eighth-floor apartment. Yet another middle school student of about fifteen in Jiading District was stopped when he attempted to jump off a school building on the same day. He was distraught because he was held back in the same grade for another year due to poor academic performance. The next day, the thirteen-year-old in Changning District jumped to his death. 'Since when did thirteen-year-olds begin to seek escape from life? Are they children at all?' Wu Jiayin opined.

Even though we had been in Shanghai for such a short time, we understood that it was unlikely the pressure on students in go-ahead China would change. With so many students in the system, competition from an early age was always going to be fierce and rank would be judged on basic criteria like exam results. Education was usually the only ticket out of poverty – often for a student's whole family – in China. Opportunities were there for the winners. High academic achievers in China were feted like sports stars in Australia. There is no safety net for those who don't make the cut. Students and their parents are driven to do whatever it takes to get ahead of the rest. The system was also complicit in perpetuating the problem. From elementary school on, nearly all teachers were subjected to quantitative assessment, which meant class test results were linked to teachers' earnings. The columnist Wan Lixin said many teachers and parents were aware that this pedagogy was destroying children both mentally and physically. 'But even the most liberal-minded teachers dare not do what's right for the kids, encumbered as they are by their own big family to support,' he said.

I realise the concerns I had over the private kindergartens for my kids in Shanghai were nowhere near as significant as the issues facing students and parents in Chinese kindergartens, primary and high schools. From what I saw, I was extremely thankful that my kids were not going to be battling their entire schooling career to stand out in the Chinese education system. But I also think it would be hard not to have been caught up in the competitiveness had we stayed in China given the cost of private schools for expat kids and the inevitable comparisons of results to those being achieved by Chinese students. And we might have found ourselves pushing harder for them to succeed in the Chinese environment than if we were in Australia, and even wondering why we didn't start their formal education earlier. Whether an expat or a Chinese parent, we all want the best for our children and do what we think is right at the time to give them the best opportunities in life. We do it because no-one wants their child to be the one left behind.

CHAPTER 6

HAPPY NEW YEAR

Bang, it was Chinese New Year. We had been in Shanghai one month and, bang, we were on holidays.

There's nothing quite like a Chinese New Year's Eve party. It's explosive and it's deafening. It's like Shanghai is trying to blow itself up.

Chinese New Year, or Spring Festival, is the most important of the traditional Chinese holidays. The festival begins on the first day of the first month of the Chinese calendar and ends on the fifteenth day, which is also the Lantern Festival. Within the Spring Festival falls a Golden Week holiday. This is a week when the country's industry virtually grinds to a standstill and the entire workforce takes a holiday. It is the time of the world's greatest human migration, when millions of migrant workers return to their home towns and provinces for family celebrations and reunions.

China introduced Golden Week holidays in 1999. The main motivation behind stamping a whole week for a national holiday was to encourage locals to spend. China's National Bureau of Statistics says the first 19 Golden Weeks contributed A$105 billion to the economy as workers were able to get out and see their own tourist sites and indulge in holiday spending. It is really the only time many Chinese workers get holidays. Workers' rights, especially regarding compensation and holidays, are not among the highest priorities in China. The Communist Party-backed All-China Federation of Trade Unions says that China has 209 million trade union members and the organisation is involved in a raft of laws and regulations designed to protect worker rights. However, Chinese workers, particularly migrant workers, reportedly often work in poor or dangerous conditions for minimal pay. So when Golden Week arrives, no-one is prepared to miss out on going home or having a good time.

Chinese New Year in 2008, the Year of the Rat – or after much discussion at the *Shanghai Daily* over the attributes of rats and mice, The Year of the Mouse – fell on February 7. The Chinese year follows the lunar calendar. A lunar year is made up of twelve months with 29-and-a-half days in each month. An extra month is added every now and then, creating a lunar leap year, to synchronise with the solar calendar. The Chinese calendar counts years in cycles of 60. Each year has dual labels. One is for the celestial stem, or one of the five elements of wood, fire, earth, metal and water. The year is also labelled according to the terrestrial branch, which is one of the twelve animal signs. Every twelve-year sequence the animals take on one of the elements until all five have been used, hence the 60-year cycle. The Year of the Earth Rat was 2008.

New Year festivities start on the first day of the first month of each Chinese year, or the fall of the New Moon, and continue for fifteen days, when the moon is at its brightest. It is two weeks of feasting and family and fun. It is a time of great tradition. In the week ahead of New Year, families spend countless hours cleaning. They can't use a broom again until the fifth day of the New Year as doing so before then is believed to sweep good luck out of the family. They put a piece of red paper with the Chinese character for happiness upside down on the door. This means happiness has arrived. Everyone wears red to scare away evil spirits. 'Red is the colour of the sun, the fire and the blood,' Zhong Fulan, a professor of Chinese folk culture at East China Normal University, tells the *Shanghai Daily*. 'Red represents success, loyalty and justice. It is also believed to be the colour that brings people good luck.' Red underwear is especially popular. When someone's *ben ming nian* arrives – when the sign of the year is the same as their birth sign – it is supposed to be a year of bad luck and unpredictable illness. Wearing red, especially close to the skin, wards off bad luck. Red lingerie and red thermal underwear always sells fast close to New Year.

During the festive season families feast on fish for abundance and hot pot, which is like a Chinese fondue, and make dumplings (*jiaozi*) which are similar in shape to the old currency of gold ingots. Having many dumplings symbolises that the family will make a fortune.

On the fifteenth day, the Lantern Festival is held. We couldn't wait to take the kids to the parades, the lion and dragon dances, taste the famous dumplings and *tangyuan*, the small dumpling ball of glutinous rice and stuffed with fillings of sesame, bean paste, jujube paste and walnut meat. And we were looking forward to seeing all the lanterns. The most popular Lantern Festival legend says the Jade Emperor in heaven was so angered with the people in a particular town for killing his favourite goose that he decided to destroy the town with fire. A good-hearted fairy heard of the awful plan and warned the townsfolk to light lanterns, tricking the Jade Emperor into thinking the town was ablaze. Since then, lanterns are carried through the streets on the first full moon of the year. We planned to go down to the old town and the area around Shanghai's Yuyuan Gardens. The bazaar is always vibrant and lively and the gardens are famous for being illuminated with 10 000 lanterns during the festival. Yuyuan Gardens is one of Shanghai's landmarks, a classical Chinese garden built 400 years ago during the Ming Dynasty. It is full of zigzagging bridges and paths with peepholes, windows, doorways and gazebos opening onto intricate rock formations, sculptures, and a winding dragon wall – literally a wall that looks just like a dragon – that seems never-ending. The hubbub of the bazaar outside offsets the serenity within the garden walls where blooming fruit trees and ornamental pools pop up through arches and around corners in delightful splashes of colour. Adjoining Yuyuan Gardens is the Huxinting teahouse, famous for hosting Queen Elizabeth II and Bill Clinton on respective trips to Shanghai. The teahouse sits in the middle of a goldfish-filled lake and you can only reach it by the Bridge of Nine Turns. The bends on the bridge are to stop evil spirits, which apparently can't take corners. At one end of the bridge is also the Nanxiang Steamed Dumplings restaurant, famous for the Shanghai specialty *xiao long bao*. The dumplings are usually filled with pork but there is also a version stuffed with fresh crab roe. On the occasion we did make it across the bridge, which took close to an hour and left us squashed and breathless from the crowds of tour groups following red and yellow flags or umbrellas or scarves or pom-poms, we decided the Nanxiang queue was far too long, regardless of how good the dumplings might be. We ducked into another restaurant a few doors away offering 'dumpling of crad (sic) ovaries'. They were really quite tasty.

With all of this on offer, we couldn't understand at all why the few expat friends we had made had planned to leave Shanghai and China for the Golden Week, or had already left telling us they would return after the national holiday. We figured they'd be missing a whole lot of fun.

We soon learned that fun at New Year in China comes predominantly in the form of fireworks. Fireworks and firecrackers are the celebratory tools of choice across the city. Historically used to ward off evil spirits, Shanghai constantly bangs with fireworks. Anyone can buy them. Anyone can set them off. Anywhere. There are never more fireworks set off than at Chinese New Year, and nowhere more than in Shanghai.

Looking out of our windows, we noticed a fireworks stall being set up on Changle Lu, right in front of a convenience store on the intersection of Xinzha Lu. The crackers were rolled up in red paper and strung on a long fuse wire in batches seemingly numbering up to 100. There were more and more customers as New Year approached. We were excited, although a little concerned as the children both had an expressed fear of fireworks. When Nelson was nine months old, we took the children to a fireworks display at a special summertime kids' fair. Perhaps the only sound louder than the fireworks popping over the Tweed River in northern New South Wales was Nelson's screams of terror, which then sparked empathetic Milly to burst into wails of panic and alarm, totally at odds with the beauty of the illuminations in the sky. We slunk away from the children's Christmas party day all quite distressed. Now in Shanghai there was no escape, but we reasoned that they were older and we could talk them through all the excitement and hope it didn't dredge up some memory of previous trauma.

And so it started. It went on for two whole weeks. Every night, groups of men (we thought it was the concierge/security types from our complex) would set off firecrackers for a solid five or six hours. They'd set off a bundle. Run to the shop, buy more. Set them off. Buy more. Set them off. They set them off on the street corner, in the middle of the road, at the bus stop and, unable to contain their excitement, just metres from the fireworks stall. Their merry-making wasn't restricted to the evening. They'd have little practices during the day as well, starting about 8 a.m. These were grown men. They weren't yahooing, drinking, or causing a disturbance on the ground while admiring their latest crackling effort. They were just standing around in the freezing conditions letting off fireworks, and then letting off more. For hours.

My eyes and ears had never been subject to quite the same assault as during the crazy fortnight of Chinese New Year in Shanghai. New Year's Eve and the fifth day of the New Year were the worst. Huge blasts that sounded like cannon fire would boom out from our street corner about 7 p.m. – a colourful harbinger of the display to come. Each night the children, winding down towards bedtime, would hear the firework bangs and run screaming to hide behind the couch. After the initial blaze, the zippy fireworks would start, sounding like machine gun fire. Then the really colourful ones would start, mixed with zippy ones and cannon fire. We would watch them from the windows of our apartment. It happens that the 20th storey is precisely the height at which many fireworks explode. We'd seen the notices posted around our building that kindly wished us a happy New Year and oddly warned us to close all the windows and turn the gas off. Now we understood why. The fireworks exploded right outside our windows. The crackers that looked so close you could touch them, actually were. The building shuddered with each blast. The flashes left scorch marks on our outside walls, fizzing cinders landed on our tiny balcony, and firework fragments bounced off our windows.

We didn't think it was quite the way to help get the kids over their firework phobia. Yet, there is something to be said about facing one's fears. Each night, the hazy night sky would suddenly come alight. The interior of our apartment would light up to match, changing from purple to gold to red to green. There could be no hiding from the vibrant onslaught. Amid the crackling and banging and the multi-coloured glow, the wails behind the couch began to subside. By about the third sleepless night it was replaced by the wacky, unbridled joy of children witnessing an awesome spectacle. The television was switched off – even on full volume, we couldn't hear it anyway. All four of us pressed our faces up against the window glass, seeing who would be the first to flinch at the fiery bursts, which colour our apartment would be bathed in first, second and third, how many crackers would go off in one volley, and when the frenzy subsided around 2 a.m. or 3 a.m., how much firework rubbish would be left on the streets. You just can't have that kind of fun in Australia. That's because it's illegal, except in Darwin in the country's deep north, where almost anything goes and they have the occasional day when it's legal to buy and set off as many fireworks as you can handle.

In the end we didn't see any of the Chinese New Year parades or dances or 10 000 lanterns. We didn't manage go out much at all. When we did, it was with the wobbly walk of the sleep-deprived and the nervousness of people who never know when or where the next round of crackers will fire. We did dream of blowing up entire firework stalls to the cheers of parents everywhere. And we did vow, should we be based in Shanghai for the next Chinese New Year, to flee the country and head anywhere offering peace and quiet.

And then it was over. On the fifteenth day, we slept. And the children moaned: 'But where are the fireworks?'

CHAPTER 7

SNOWED IN

It was so cold in Shanghai. Snow was falling and the city looked clean. I foud myself staring out of our window, struck by how lovely the building site diagonally opposite looked in the early morning, the flashes of a welder's torch spotlighting fresh snow cover and reflecting off the yellow hardhats of the workers. The dull grey of pollution cover was erased from rooftops all around. In its place was a pristine sheen. Looking down upon the wintry vision I saw it punctuated by cyclists in bold coloured raincoats looking like hundreds and thousands on fairy bread. I thought it was utterly lovely and took the children outside to make snowmen in our garden. They had, by this time, acquired mittens and snow jackets with hoods, yet we still attracted tut-tuts from gardeners and other hardy souls who were braving the conditions to walk their dogs. It was the pampered pooches brought out of the compact apartments for their daily walks that appeared to be the most snug among us in their jackets and scarves. The dogs even had tiny booties.

The snow in Shanghai was unusual. It seems I have been blessed by good luck when it comes to happening upon places experiencing unusual weather conditions. I recall how 'lucky' I was to be at Uluru in central Australia in 1997, the only time in living memory that it has snowed on the famous outback rock. Expecting the sun to be beating down on the red dirt and mulga, I was ill-prepared for the base temperature of five degrees Celsius, sloppy sleet and rain. On another occasion, I travelled to Australia's famous salt-crusted dry lake, Lake Eyre. I arrived with it in flood. The muddy film of water across the lake was a far cry from the rock-hard salt plain where land speed record attempts are regularly staged. Of course it could be far worse, but I wonder why my luck never sees me arrive anywhere experiencing strangely agreeable conditions and unexpected pleasantness.

In Shanghai, it was snowing by the bucket load. The children had never before seen snow. We caught snowflakes, got the ice caught in our hair, on our faces, and up our sleeves. We left gum-booted footprints in the crunchy ice, threw and dodged compacted snowballs and picked at the ice-covered ponds to see if we could catch any snap-frozen goldfish. I forbade the children to catch any falling snow on their tongues – the delicate snowflakes may have looked white but they had sludged through layers of pollution to reach us. Then, despite my concerns over cleanliness, I got caught up in the thrill of the moment and rushed off with the kids to find frozen snails to help decorate their snowman.

It felt like it had been snowing for weeks. On February 1 and 2 the heaviest snowstorms for 60 years hit the city. Most areas were blanketed in more than 10 cm of snow. Chongming County, neighbouring Shanghai's suburban sprawl, recorded 21 cm, while the Xujiahui area in Xuhui District had 5 cm. Then the snow stopped. But only for a day. The one-day break was enormously good news in Shanghai. It meant passengers and cargo delayed by the heavy snow were able to leave the city by air and by road. It was the start of gradually clearing conditions that the Shanghai Meteorological Bureau said would see the weather for the Spring Festival Golden Week turn sunny with occasional clouds. The bureau predicted temperatures in downtown areas would be a relatively comfortable minus two degrees Celsius and minus three or four degrees in the suburbs. Maximum temperatures would be around five degrees.

Shanghai was lucky. The worst of the deadliest snowstorms to hit China in 50 years missed the city. It meant I was able to go out and play in the snow with the kids and consider the snowfalls a bit of fun. It meant we could enjoy the Golden Week, our worries confined to the impact of fireworks on our sleep. Millions of Chinese weren't so lucky. We soon realised how fortunate we were to be in Shanghai and how insulated we were from the national disaster that played out around us, causing stress and suffering on a massive scale.

Heavy snow had been falling across the south, centre and east of China from mid-January, leading to road closures, flight cancellations and hordes of passengers swarming railway stations. Millions of people were trying to return to their homes for the traditional Spring

Festival. The country's transport system was at breaking point. Railways were running non-stop. On January 21 alone, trains across the country transported more than 4.2 million passengers desperate to get home for the Golden Week break. But January 21 wasn't the busiest day. Shanghai Railways was bracing to carry 178.6 million passengers during the travel rush from January 23 to March 2.

By January 29, the *Shanghai Daily* reported at least 24 people had died in the ice storms and hundreds of thousands were stranded. It said ten people had been killed by their houses collapsing under snow. Another ten died after slipping on icy streets. Two people had drowned and another two were killed by falling trees.

The snowstorms affected 77.87 million people in the provinces of Anhui, Jiangxi, Henan, Hunan, Hubei, Guangxi, Sichuan, Guizhou, Yunnan, Shaanxi, Gansu and Qinghai. Chongqing Municipality and Xinjiang Uygur Autonomous Region were also hit by heavy snow. More than 827 000 people had been relocated after more than 107 000 houses collapsed during the weeks of blizzard conditions. Another 399 000 houses had been damaged. About 4.3 million hectares of crops had also been destroyed by the falls and the snow had caused a direct economic loss of 22.09 billion yuan (A\$3.6 billion) to the country.

As the crisis grew, China Premier Wen Jiabao headed to the snow-bound city of Changsha to address thousands of stranded passengers. 'I am deeply apologetic that you are stranded in the railway station and not able to go home earlier,' Wen told the crowd through a megaphone. 'When the electricity network is back, then the trains can run and it will not be long before you can all go back home to celebrate the New Year.' Wen's visit to the chaotic scene was carried in print and on television internationally. The magnitude of the snowstorm suffering was beginning to be realised.

Into the third week of the storms, whole cities had been blacked out, the entire Chinese transport system had been paralysed and millions of people were stuck in railway stations and terminals or make-shift shelters. At least 53 people had died. The 4.6 million residents of Chenzhou City in Hunan Province had had no power or running water for six days. Shops and banks had closed, hospitals and government buildings were without power and communication lines had been damaged by the snow.

Then the storm eased and the stampede to catch the restored train services began. In the newspapers and on television I saw the terrified faces of toddlers caught up in the mad charge for transportation, and women crying and fainting in the crush. There were no riots or outbreaks of violence, just a forceful rush onto trains by people who had been stuck for days in cramped, standing room only conditions, unable to sleep, with inadequate protection against the cold, minimal food and water. They had been waiting there all this time because many couldn't get home. But most just didn't want to miss out on their holiday.

A month after the storms began to inflict their misery, the *Shanghai Daily* reported 60 people were dead. The Civil Affairs Ministry said the snowstorms had caused a direct economic loss to the country of 53.8 billion yuan (A$8.7 billion). At least 1.76 million people had had to relocate and 5.8 million people had been stranded at stations nationwide. We thought things were starting to improve. But the storms were not done yet.

Savage storms returned across the country throughout February. The death toll climbed to 129. While transport lines reopened, authorities battled to repair power lines and ensure food supplies after millions of hectares of crops suffered damage and more than 70 million animals perished. More than 1.66 million people displaced by the winter freeze remained in temporary shelters. Areas that escaped the snow didn't escape the disaster's reach. Food prices were driven up across the country. Inflation surged to an eleven-year high of 7.1 per cent. China suffered 151 billion yuan (A$24.4 billion) in economic losses.

Those who weren't stuck in the chaos or among the millions without power were lucky. Despite the snow, many of the country's workers managed to get home for a holiday. And, with the holiday season over, they returned to the cities for work. It stopped snowing, but the impact of the snowstorms lingered. The human toll of the blizzards still ticked upwards and cities still struggled without full power, running water or communication lines. Transport lines around the country remained cut or damaged. The tide of people wanting to get home or return from holiday may no longer have been swamping train and bus stations and airports, but vital food and cargo still could not get through. Coal and power supplies throughout China were stretched to their limits. The price of food around the country had risen significantly and would stay high for the next few months after so many crops were destroyed by the icy onslaught.

The price rises made massive inroads into already stretched family budgets. We too felt the impact of the price hikes. While our incomes were not high by Australian standards, we were earning significantly more than the average Chinese professional. Again, it meant we couldn't really appreciate how hard people had been hit by the snowstorms. Despite living in China, our lives were segregated from many Chinese. We hadn't been caught up in the snow chaos, we had no family or friends affected by the storms. All we knew of the disaster was what we could access in the English-language news. We were able to retreat to the safety and warmth of our apartment after having a wonderful time playing in the falling snow. We might have felt a bit cold and sleepless during our Golden Week, but we returned to work after the holiday thankful we had decided to stay put in Shanghai. And just a little bit more aware of how privileged our lives were in China.

CHAPTER 8

IT'S NEWSPAPERS, BUT NOT AS WE KNOW IT

I was to be a 'foreign expert'. My job, as it had been outlined to me, was working on the *Shanghai Daily*, the city's only English-language daily newspaper, rewriting and editing copy for grammar, punctuation, clarity, accuracy, fairness, wordiness, completeness, poor organisation and other writing errors. I was to identify libellous or potentially libellous stories, identify those that needed major revision, assist in coaching some of the writers by answering questions on style or grammar, and write headlines. The bulk of my job, I had been told, would be converting 'Chinglish', written by the Chinese journalists who were writing in their second – or sometimes third or fourth – language, into English. It really meant quite intensive sub-editing. I was one of eight foreign experts working on the night desk when I commenced. My hours were from about 4.30 p.m. through until my last page was signed off – anywhere between 11.30 p.m. and 1.30 a.m. I had used some of the time since we'd arrived to study the paper and analyse where I thought improvements could be made. I showed up to work full of the required 'spirit of friendly cooperation' and was keen to get involved and impart any knowledge I could to assist in the production of the newspaper.

The *Shanghai Daily* was founded in March, 1999 and the newspaper's first office was on the 10th and 11th floors of the Wenhui Mansion on the Bund where journalists enjoyed great views of the famous strip, Pudong, and the tugboats on the Huangpu River. The building was once home to the office of the *Wenhui Daily*, one of the oldest Shanghai-based Chinese language newspapers. In August 1999, the *Shanghai Daily* moved to the Wenhui-Xinmin United Press Tower on Weihai Road. Like so many buildings and landmarks in Shanghai, the Wenhui Mansion has been demolished.

The *Shanghai Daily* sells about 30 000 copies a day, according to a recent managing editor. It publishes seven days a week. I am told the readership is about a 50-50 split between expats and English-speaking Chinese. It is run by the Wenhui-Xinmin United Press Group, which controls editorial. The Group reports to the Shanghai municipal government and the Communist Party's Propaganda Department that oversees the city's media. Australia's Kerry Stokes, through his company Australian Capital Equity, had a significant stake in the paper in 2008, with direction largely over advertising and marketing – although a spokesperson for Australian Capital

Equity said she would neither confirm nor deny the company's involvment in the Chinese publication.

From the moment I arrived, I realised I had never, in almost 20 years of journalism, seen a newspaper organised in the manner of the *Shanghai Daily*. The newsroom appeared to operate without a point person known as a chief-of-staff or news editor to monitor the selection of stories and progression of stories throughout the day. This meant important stories could be missed entirely, or stories may have glaring omissions or problems, but the journalist had often gone home by the time their article was checked. This system, however, did give journalists a great deal of autonomy in covering a story and deciding what was newsworthy.

In the production phase of the paper, various Chinese 'chiefs', many of whom were not actually journalists, were in charge of designing a page and placing stories onto it. They then checked off the page when the stories had all been subbed and headlined by a foreign expert. It was a system which did give very hands-on control of entire pages to an individual chief and therefore was a good way of ensuring one person was accountable for page quality. But it could also lead to the same story appearing on different pages of the same edition of the paper. Stories that had appeared in the paper days earlier could also find their way back into print when they were chosen by a different chief. There was no cohesiveness to the way news was presented, even when the paper was tackling a big event.

The foreign experts on the newspaper learned very early on that the words or pages that they worked on were always subject to at least another review before publication by a Chinese chief or editor determined to put their own stamp on the work. Unfortunately, it meant some mistakes could sneak back onto pages. A final check was also carried out by the editor and an assistant editor who acted as the eyes of the Communist Party to confirm the content was in line with the Central Party Propaganda Department directives.

It was these final tweaks that often led to hilarious results. One of the more famous cases of such a late change, as told to me by Bernie Leo, involved a story about a Hong Kong film star who died and whose funeral was being held the following day. The *Shanghai Daily* headline initially read: '...(starlet) to be laid to rest today'. The page that went to press after it was altered by an assistant editor carried the headline: '...(starlet) to be laid today'.

Smarty also suffered a change to a headline he wrote that drastically altered the tone of a story. The story told of the breathtaking beauty of mountainous Tibet, but it also revealed a terrible side effect of living in the region. The incidence of heart disease, especially among children, had been found to be growing rapidly in the high altitude. To compound the problem, few doctors were available in the area. Smarty headlined the double-page feature story: 'Tibetan children pay price for living the high life.' After it left his hands, the story was remade on to a single page and, without any foreign expert getting to check the final version, carried the headline: 'Tibetan kids pay price for living'.

Starting a new job can be a little awkward and it often takes some time to settle in. I began at the newspaper a couple of weeks after Smarty and a couple of months after the other most recent arrival on the foreign experts' desk. While the paper's senior management is Chinese, foreign experts from America, Canada, the United Kingdom, Australia, Singapore and India have been part of the newspaper's make-up since it was launched. The foreign experts were sprinkled throughout the various departments, but it turned out we all shared a similar experience. By the end of my first week, I had a few headlines changed by a Chinese 'chief' for reasons I was unable to decipher and realised that while I had questioned a few of the facts in stories and sought more information on others, my queries generally went nowhere. I had struggled to rewrite some of the stories as the basic information that was conventionally required – names, dates, locations – was just not available and the journalists said they had no way of finding it out as they did not talk to anybody while writing the story. I also learned that in court cases dealing with allegations of rape, often it is the victim – even if the victim is a child – who is named in China. Perhaps to lessen my shock, I was told that sometimes it is not the victim's real name that is released, but a name made up by police. I argued that in a country of almost 1.4 billion people, there was a good chance someone goes by that name and may not be pleased to be falsely identified as a victim of rape.

On the newspaper some reporters were assigned to do translations, which meant they rewrote stories that appeared in the Chinese media so they could appear in the English-language publication. I soon found that it was often stories that had occurred in Shanghai that were being translated. This meant that *Shanghai Daily* readers were often only made aware of events happening in Shanghai days or weeks after they had happened, and also after they had appeared in other newspapers or on other websites. I tried suggesting ways to encourage the reporters to unearth stories that hadn't already been published elsewhere or arrived on a press release, but got no response (like all the other foreign experts who suggested a similar plan before me).

I did, however, get some feedback on my work. I was pulled up over allowing the occasional British, rather than the newspaper's approved American style and spelling through. I took it as a legitimate criticism of my work, but despaired about the bigger picture changes that could make a huge difference to the quality of the newspaper and perhaps make it a bit more interesting and appealing to more readers.

I was left feeling somewhat confused by the arrangement I had entered into. Smarty couldn't help laughing at my astonishment. He had had a little longer to work through his frustrations. Hired for his newspaper design expertise, he said he had not had one page he had designed make it into the paper unchanged. My foreign expert colleagues agreed they had also been through the same workplace shock, but had swallowed their professional pride and had become accustomed to the requirements of the job and the accepted practices on the newspaper. We all realised soon enough that we could learn a lot from our 'expert' posting, even if it was a study in working co-operatively in a foreign environment and identifying the methods that were not conducive to what we considered quality journalism.

It was quite an odd feeling I experienced as I walked to work each day. Rather than heading into work as informed of the day's events as possible and carrying suggestions or ideas to pursue, my preparation was to talk myself down from interfering or offering advice. The environment I'd enter was also atypical of newspapers. On walking into the office for the evening shift, which is when a newspaper is usually at its most lively, I found I was entering a quiet zone. Reporters were rarely on the telephone. Often they'd come into the office, slip off their shoes and put on a pair of slippers, turn up their humidifier machines and prepare their cups of tea with herbs, extracts and goji berries. Many stayed at their computer terminals throughout the day, re-writing information that came into the newspaper from approved sources or, occasionally, adding extra research from the Internet. As reporters rarely went out to talk to people or cover news, photographers didn't go with them to capture news pictures. This meant photographers attended events or roamed the city to take photographs that were really only used to fill in holes in the newspaper.

Sometimes reporters did attend press conferences. 'Red envelopes' were offered at press conferences and media events. I was told that reporters regularly accepted red envelopes – literally red envelopes containing wads of cash – to attend the press conferences and get the stories in the paper. If a reporter got the story a good run in the paper, they were invited to the next event where another red envelope would be in the offing. Those that took the cash but did not get the story much of a run did not get a return invite. It was an accepted practice in China. I was not convinced such blatant bribery really happened until one expat colleague working as a reporter at the paper found himself in a position where he felt obliged to accept a red envelope. He felt so ethically compromised, he donated it to charity. An expat publicist for an international hotel also told a number of the foreign newspaper staff of her red envelope experience. As one of her first events in the job, she said she hosted a function for the opening of a new champagne bar. Food and drinks were laid on for the media announcement. However, she was told free drinks were not what was required in China and local reporters would not attend unless they received red envelopes. Journalists not showing up for free food and alcohol? She, and we, were incredulous.

Uninvited, and therefore without the issue of red envelopes to deal with, I took the chance to attend a press conference in Shanghai for a story I was doing on organ transplants in China. The main talent was the vice minister of China's Ministry of Health, Huang Jiefu. I was doing a profile on Huang Jiefu and was looking to interview him after he finished the press conference. A liver disease and transplant specialist, Huang was at the forefront of promoting legal and ethical organ transplants in China. Each year in China, more than 1 million people die of organ failure. Only 10 000 people each year undergo lifesaving transplant operations. The shortfall is largely due to the lack of organs. The discrepancy between supply and demand has created a legal, ethical and moral quagmire on the issue of organ transplants in China. Huang acknowledged that the majority of organs used in transplants in China come from executed prisoners. The system had long been subjected to questions over how freely death row prisoners provide the consent for their organs to be harvested, whether the available organs are distributed on the basis of need or the ability to pay, and the prevalence of organ trading.

Huang Jiefu said there was only one way to fix the problem. He wanted more organs. He was using the press conference to encourage people to become organ donors. It was a tough task. Health experts opined that if organs were allowed to be taken from people who were 'brain dead', it would certainly increase the organ supply. But the Chinese people's belief that they live until their last breath has stopped them from donating organs and permitting organs to be harvested from people who are brain dead. In China, the three main tenets of the culture are Buddhism, Confucianism and Taoism. 'Our task is to get people to say that donating their organs is consistent with the principles of these three elements of the culture,' Huang said.

Huang and five other experts delivered their latest findings and statistical research into organ donation to the packed press conference. It was all in Chinese so I couldn't understand anything and was especially concerned I would miss the most important information that inevitably comes when the journalists get to ask questions after the presentations. I need not have worried. To my surprise, there were no questions. As the last speaker finished, the journalists broke into a round of applause. They then dutifully got up and went back to their offices to file stories on the information they were provided. There was not one question. There was not one follow-up interview request. Just clapping. At least I got a full five minutes alone with Huang Jiefu at the end of the press conference to do a rush interview for my feature story. Given the time constraints, I felt I needed to be quite forward in steering him away from statistics and figures and onto the more personal topics I needed covered. It was especially tricky in China given the heightened need for deference and preservation of 'face' that's required in such an exchange. I had no idea about the correct protocols, but adopted my most polite manner in the hope I wouldn't make too many culturally insensitive mistakes in my questioning. Huang Jiefu, however, seemed pleased to talk off-script and enjoyed telling anecdotes of his career and some of the lives of Chinese people he had saved by performing liver transplants. He also told me he trained for a time in Australia at the national liver transplant centre connected to Sydney's Royal Prince Alfred Hospital. If we'd had the time I'd have liked to have talked to him about the differences he saw in health care – and the media – between the two countries.

The *Shanghai Daily* is not newspapers as we know it. It is not newspapers as the West knows it. The editors say they aspire to be like '*The Times of London*'. Alas, the paper's obsession with weather reports is the only thing that gives it the slight flavour of a British newspaper. There are occasional stories, especially out of the courts, that are really interesting. Otherwise the content is low on information and high on rhetoric. Many of my Chinese friends wryly note that according to the newspaper, nothing bad ever happens in Shanghai.

A lot of the content of the *Shanghai Daily*, and most other publications in China, comes from the Beijing-based, government-approved media service, Xinhua. Xinhua copy is a bit hit and miss. One memorable example I encountered came from the enormous number of stories from Xinhua sent on one of the bigger events of the year in China – the nation's first space-walk. On September 27, millions of Chinese watched as *taikonaut* (astronaut) Zhai Zhigang made history with a 20-minute space walk. The feat made China the third country, after Russia and the United States, to successfully send a man on a spacewalk. Zhai, 42, became a national hero when he emerged from the capsule, beamed live to ground control and onto television sets throughout the nation, followed by teammate Liu Boming, who also briefly emerged from Shenzhou VII to hand Zhai a Chinese national flag to wave in outer space. The mission's third crew member, Jing Haipeng, remained in the spacecraft. In a story written to add a bit of colour to the event, Xinhua sent through a piece describing the conditions inside the module: 'A wide variety of seasoning sauces, but a less diverse colors of furniture and decoration inside the module. The three Chinese taikonauts who began their mission Thursday evening will have flavored but, perhaps, not that colorful days in outer space. Above all, however, the men will surely boast the convenience of a toilet that was a luxury their predecessors might dreamed of in the previous two missions.' It is not easy to make words like that sing.

In the task of rewriting copy, I found it was often in the direct translations into English that the subtleties and niceties of the language could be lost. Sometimes they got messed up completely. We didn't quite know what to say when a story came through to be subbed with the intro: 'A woman woke up screaming inside her muffin.' The poor woman was in fact afraid she'd been buried alive and was screaming inside a coffin.

Health and medical stories often required finessing. On a regular basis, I was presented with paragraphs like: 'Children's spraying vomit and a sudden growth of the head can be syndromes of brain tumor, which is ranked the second most common pediatric tumor in the nation, experts said on a national pediatric neurosurgery forum in the city yesterday.'

Sometimes, though, the Chinese approach, unencumbered by fancy writing and euphemism and with an ancient adage often thrown in, added its own special touch to a story. We decided that we just had to leave a story that began: 'Love always has its cost and for a college student in east China's Zhejiang Province, the cost was that he was almost engulfed by raging sea waves after pledging that he would never leave a typhoon-ravaged beach until his girlfriend showed up.'

I found there were a lot of reasons to enjoy working at the *Shanghai Daily* and, despite our grumbles, Smarty and I were grateful for our jobs. The work might have been a challenge to our own professionalism and understanding of how we thought the media should operate, but it did provide a valuable insight into how news is delivered in China. To enjoy our time in Shanghai and extract the most we could from our working environment after bringing our family so far, we realised we must operate within the system. Besides, it was not easy to get permanent employment in China. Locals could find it immensely difficult and needed to present all types of credentials to secure jobs. I found a story in the *Shanghai Daily* that I kept with me for the next time I heard how hard it was to get a job in Australia or fantasised about tossing in the job and taking my chances in the Chinese job market. It said Chinese employers had begun rejecting job seekers based on their horoscope or blood type instead of experience and ability. Workers with blood type A or AB, for example, were generally in with a chance at a job as they were considered careful in their work or good at communication. The tests had also been used to help bosses weed out contenders whose horoscope was incompatible with the employer's own. I read that, fortunately, lawyers and human resources experts had weighed in to help the workers. According to the story, the word from the experts was that: 'Blood type might be related to a job seeker's personality, but it can only be considered as a reference and should not be the reason an employer turns down an applicant'.

CHAPTER 9

THE TIBET SITUATION

Chinese people love to read newspapers. Newspapers are posted page-by-page in big glass cabinets around the city near parks where people can read them. Taxi drivers grab every break in traffic, every traffic light, to devour the news. There is a phenomenon I noticed of people reading while walking – students reading text books, women reading magazines, and everybody reading newspapers. Remarkably, even on footpaths crowded with readers, nobody bumps into anyone else.

Newspapers in China are bucking a worldwide trend and are actually growing in popularity and readership. China's newspaper sales increased 3.84 per cent from 2007 to 2008 and were up

20.69 per cent over the five years to 2008, according to World
Association of Newspapers figures. There are more than 2200
newspapers in China. It is the world's largest market for daily
newspapers with 107 million copies sold daily in 2007, followed by
India with 99 million, Japan with 68 million, the United States with
almost 51 million, and Germany with 20.6 million. There are 39
newspaper groups in China, including Wenhui-Xinmin United Press
Group, Beijing Daily Newspaper Group, and Guangzhou Daily
Newspaper Group. The *Shanghai Daily* is just one of the newspapers
on offer in Shanghai.

Television is also viewed on a massive scale in China. There are
13 specialised television channels in Shanghai. Before China
launched its reform and opening up policy in 1978, people received
only two TV news reports a day. There are now channels devoted to
news and live updates, making the delivery of television news and
programming 'more diversified, open and transparent', according to
local commentators.

I didn't have the television on much at home, though I considered
putting on the children's programs shown on CCTV7 and Oriental
Youth Channel to help the kids pick up some songs and words in
Mandarin. Unfortunately the children's shows all seemed to be
scheduled for late evening – perhaps when Chinese children could
watch TV after they'd finally come home from school and had done
their homework. I didn't watch the local news. Rather, I took my TV
news from the broadcasts of CNN that were not blacked out by
censors.

Shanghai television came to life on October 1, 1958. We were in
Shanghai as the city celebrated 50 years of television. For the

medium's 50-year anniversary, the city's first television reporters gave a history of their experience delivering Shanghai TV news. It was better than anything I'd seen on the box in China all year. The reporters, Zhu Dun and Zou Zhimin, recounted how the cameras they used to make the broadcast were borrowed from a film studio and a thrift shop. They said they realised soon after filming that they didn't have film developing technicians. So they resorted to an X-ray unit at a local hospital to make the city's first TV newsreel. They also described how their skills were quite different to modern-day TV newshounds. In the early days they not only had to film the stories, they had to carry the heavy cameras around on bamboo poles or on a tricycle to get to events. Of course news gathering modernised, as did funding of television in China. The Shanghai television industry sold its first advertising slot in 1979 – a 90-second commercial advertising a domestic ginseng wine. The ad triggered a run on all stocks of the liquor.

Shanghai television's light entertainment didn't seem that different to what we have in the West. The local television I did watch was late at night when I managed to sneak in a foot massage on my way home from work. If I could make it into the Beijing Xie Lu parlour just after midnight, I could sit back and relax while I got an hour-long foot soak and massage for 45 yuan (A$7). None of the girls spoke English and, as there were generally few customers so late at night, there was little conversation. Instead we all watched the television that was tuned to their favourite soap operas. I found myself getting quite hooked on a show which seemed to be about a pampered rich girl who had fallen in love with a boy from the wrong side of the tracks. In a secondary, and less glamorous storyline, the girl's grandmother kept having flashbacks of her youth when she too had a lover who was not acceptable to the family. Courtesy of my soap-opera watching I was able to add a few achingly lovelorn phrases to my Chinese repertoire. I didn't try them out on Smarty. My experience was that he'd ruin the moment by trying to correct my Chinese pronunciation.

Shanghai was not immune from the reality TV show phenomenon. In China, as elsewhere, television programmers were constantly trying to come up with innovative ways to grab audience share in the face of 'new media' such as the Internet and mobile phones. I noticed that reality TV was a big hit in Shanghai where there were a plethora of shows to unearth budding pop stars, dancers, fashion models, clever people, and chefs. Shanghai television also announced a whole new entertainment channel. One of its big hits was expected to be a Chinese version of the bizarre Japanese game show 'Hole in the Wall' that was apparently popular in the US. The show featured contestants clad in spandex and hard hats who had to wriggle through various holes cut in a moving Styrofoam fence. I was not sure it would tempt me or my Chinese foot massagers away from our Chinese soaps.

As full of fun as some of the media was, television and newspapers in China still remained tools of the government. Once I had been able to reconcile in my mind that my role at work was short-term and that I could not expect the *Shanghai Daily* to be like a newspaper as we know it in the West, I found working at an organisation controlled by the government quite extraordinary. The newspaper was unashamedly used to control information on events including an uprising in Tibet ahead of the Beijing Olympic Games.

Tibet was militarily taken by China in 1951. In early March 2008, hundreds of monks marched in the Tibetan capital Lhasa to mark the 49th anniversary of the failed 1959 uprising against Chinese rule that caused the Dalai Lama, the spiritual leader of Tibetan Buddhism, to flee to India. The region has remained a constant source of unrest for China with relations antagonistic between the Communist Party and the exiled Dalai Lama. About 50 of the protesting monks, reported internationally to have been demanding the government ease rules on 'patriotic education' which requires monks to study government propaganda and ritually denounce the Dalai Lama, were arrested. As a result, other protests erupted in Lhasa and throughout Tibet and surrounding areas, spiralling into violence on March 14.

The *Shanghai Daily*, which rarely mentions Tibet without following it with the phrase 'an inalienable part of China', ran Xinhua stories reporting protesters as attacking police with knives and stones. It also ran a story citing 'the facts' on how the Dalai Lama clique plotted and incited the Lhasa violence which killed at least 18 civilians and one police officer. The story said the facts showed that the Dalai Lama group had launched a series of campaigns to tarnish the Olympic Games in Beijing, including riots in Aba Tibetan-Qiang Autonomous Prefecture, which borders Tibet, that injured civilians and more than 200 government personnel and police on March 16.

The uprising, the broadest and most sustained against Chinese rule in almost two decades, was met with sustained media coverage in China of how Dalai Lama supporters masterminded the anti-Chinese dissent. The newspaper ran government figures of the dead and injured which differed wildly from those in foreign publications

attributed mostly to sources on the ground in Tibet. It also ran
reports on civilians in Tibet rejecting the protests and applauding the
Chinese government and the police crack down. The paper's
columnists railed against the Western media, which largely included
both sides of the unrest in their reports, for distorting and
misunderstanding the issue. They claimed the foreign coverage was
biased against the Chinese people and showed how gullible or
sinister foreign journalists were. The paper ran the line that reporters
in the West were either confused about the facts or were deliberately
supporting Tibetan separatists who were acting against the wishes of
the Chinese and Tibetan people. Internet sites and parts of CNN's
coverage were blacked out during the reporting of the riots. Without
access to alternative coverage, the state-controlled media's
propaganda-heavy information flow was potent and nationalistic and
very effective.

The paper blatantly defends China and the Chinese people,
especially when it is believed its people have been slighted by the
West. Newspapers in the West commonly campaign and stick up for
their readers, but I have never seen such a co-ordinated media
operation as during the Tibet uprising or as I did watching the
Shanghai Daily and other newspapers inflame anti-foreign sentiment
in the month-long furore over CNN commentator Jack Cafferty's
infamous 'goons and thugs' slur.

On the April 9 edition of CNN's *'The Situation Room'* program,
Cafferty responded on-air to a question by host Wolf Blitzer on the
US–Sino relationship over the past 20 years. Cafferty said: 'I don't
know if China is any different, but our relationship with China is
certainly different. We're in hock to the Chinese up to our eyeballs

because of the war in Iraq, for one thing. They're holding hundreds of billions of dollars worth of our paper. We are also running hundreds of billions of dollars' worth of trade deficits with them, as we continue to import their junk with the lead paint on them and the poisoned pet food and export, you know, jobs to places where you can pay workers a dollar a month to turn out the stuff that we're buying from Wal-Mart. So I think our relationship with China has certainly changed,' he said. 'I think they're basically the same bunch of goons and thugs they've been for the last 50 years.'

He issued a clarification of his remarks on the April 14 edition of 'The Situation Room', saying that by 'goons and thugs', he meant the Chinese government, not the Chinese people. The remarks were brash and inflammatory, but did seem quite obviously directed at the nation's leadership. Not according to the Chinese media, which ran its favourite line that the West was biased against China. The paper ran hard on the story, with Xinhua copy reflecting government outrage and columnists attacking CNN and the US for calling the Chinese people goons and thugs.

On April 16 Foreign Ministry spokeswoman Jiang Yu, using language typical of the rhetoric surrounding the issue, demanded an apology from CNN. She said: 'Cafferty used the microphone in his hands to slander China and the Chinese people, seriously violated professional ethics of journalism and human conscience.' What he did 'reflected his arrogance, ignorance and hostility towards the Chinese people, ignited indignation of Chinese home and abroad, and will be condemned by those who safeguard justice around the world. We strongly demand CNN and Cafferty himself take back the vile remarks and apologise to all Chinese people'.

The *Shanghai Daily* also ran reports on rallies and international fury at Cafferty's comments while linking the CNN smear with other examples of Western bias against China. Soon Cafferty's comments were lumped in with 'hostile' reports on Tibet independence activists' attempts to disrupt the Beijing Olympic torch relay and the 'one-sided' and 'dishonest' reporting of the unrest in China's Tibet Autonomous Region. Xu Xiaobing, a law lecturer at Shanghai Jiaotong University, was published in the *Shanghai Daily* on April 30 sending a warning under the headline 'China's righteous anger simmers over Western mudslinging, hypocrisy'. His commentary seemed to epitomise the government's sentiment over the issue. He said following the Tibet riots, Olympic torch attacks, and CNN and Cafferty's assault, 'Chinese all over the world have got a much better idea where their enemies are and how to defend their nation's dignity and honour. For those who are unhappy about the direction and speed China is moving forward, China is not going to change its course.'

Chinese commentators and bloggers flooded the Internet and social media sites condemning CNN's 'racism' and wore T-shirts with 'Shut up CNN' and 'I love China'. Lawyers filed a lawsuit against CNN claiming US$1 in damages for each Chinese person – all 1.4 billion. Pro-China and anti-foreign emotions were the highest I had experienced since we arrived in China.

In such a heightened state, there is always the potential for someone to go just a bit too far. For the foreign experts on the *Shanghai Daily* at least, the overstep came in the form of an artist keen to cash in on the anti-Western attitude. The story came through on Xinhua and, as a source of amusement for all, defused a subtle but growing gap between Chinese and non-Chinese staff. I fear I will lose some of the best bits if I don't run the story in full:

'CONCEPTUAL artist Zhao Bandi has filed a lawsuit against Dreamworks Animation and Paramount Pictures, which produced and released the animated film "Kung Fu Panda".

'The Beijing Chaoyang District People's Court accepted the suit yesterday in which Zhao demands a public apology but no financial compensation, Xinhuanet.com reported yesterday.

'The artist, who is famous for carrying toy pandas and featuring them in his work, protested at the screening of the movie and said the film exploited a national symbol. Zhao has demanded that the minutes of a producers' meeting for the animated film be made public. "I think they painted the panda's eyes green with an ulterior motive. Green eyes are somewhat evil. I have studied drawing and painters will never use green eyes to portray a kind person," Zhao told Information Times, a Guangzhou-based newspaper. "That's why I have asked them to make public the minutes of the script production. I demand an explanation." The report did not say if Zhao knew that green eyes were not uncommon among Caucasian people.

'Zhao also questioned why the panda's father was a duck. "The panda is not only a symbol for China but also for the people.

'"Making the panda's father a duck is nothing but an insult to Chinese people," he said. "I am afraid that Chinese youth in years to come will think Donald Duck was their ancestor."'

CHAPTER 10

A HELPING HAND

I'd been forced to find someone to leave the children with while I went to work. It had been the most challenging aspect of moving to China – harder than finding somewhere to live, more problematic than dealing in a foreign language or with the education system, even more alien than working for state-controlled media. Because I needed to find someone within two weeks of arriving in Shanghai, I hadn't had the luxury of time to interview different nannies, but had gone with the recommendation of the only agency that had been able to find me someone on short notice. Ralph, of a nanny agency called Yash, said he had found the nanny – called an *ayi* – for us. He said she was highly qualified and recommended.

He said she was a rare find, especially in an emergency case like ours.

The vast majority of expats and increasingly more Chinese have the help of an *ayi* (literally aunty). The cheap domestic help is considered one of the perks of living in China. Many families have an *ayi* for each of their children. Many also have a cleaning *ayi* and another cooking ayi to keep the household running. It is an affordable luxury for many expats, including single people who find they don't need to spend their own time on domestic chores. In Shanghai, an *ayi* generally costs 10-20 yuan (A$1.60-3.20) an hour.

Still doubting very much that I wanted to leave the children with anyone, I headed out in our second week in China to meet *ayi* Tina in Ralph's office somewhere in the suburbs of Shanghai. I'd dragged the kids along to give their verdict. It was cold, it was dark, I felt lost and just a little afraid as I wandered around a busy alley looking for Ralph's office. Finally I found it and headed in. Tina saw us, jumped up and grabbed the kids. She hugged them and indicated to me their lack of adequate warm clothes. Then she looked me up and down, got some water and ushered me into a seat where I sat waiting for Ralph who could speak passable English. I actually liked Tina immediately. She was about my age, seemed like a no-nonsense sort of character, didn't fuss or chatter excessively, and did not look like she would bend easily to the children's every whim. I explained to Ralph how much I could afford to pay a month. It was below Tina's asking price. She said she would have to travel more than an hour from Pudong to get to our apartment every day. She would accept the monthly rate I was offering if I covered her travel expenses on top. We negotiated. I knew from speaking to expat mothers that I had offered a relatively high monthly rate of 2000 yuan (A$326) for the five hours a day she would be working for us. She said she was highly qualified and showed me all sorts of certificates and letters of recommendation. They were in Chinese but looked official. Through Ralph she told me she was worth more than I was offering. I liked her gumption. I agreed to cover the 200 yuan public transport costs for her travel per month. We had ourselves an *ayi*.

Tina seemed pleased. The kids actually seemed quite excited. I think they were under the impression that getting an *ayi* was like getting a new toy. The problem was me. I had to get comfortable with the idea of leaving the children with a woman I barely knew and could not communicate with. I had to accept that there would be someone else in the house to see all our clutter and mess. I felt awkward that she would be there watching while I mucked about with the kids. And I felt annoyed already that she would probably be checking on me, and most likely casting a concerned eye over how I looked after my family and whether my children were wearing enough layers of clothing to meet the level of overheating that the Chinese seemed to prefer. Ralph came to our house with Tina the next day so he could help me explain her duties, my expectations, and answer any questions. I'd worked myself into quite a state and I told her that her offer to do some cleaning would be nice, but my preference was that she focus on the children and keep them happy in the few hours both Smarty and I were away from home. I told her they had only been cared for by anyone other than us on rare occasions, and that she had an enormous responsibility. I told her we would try to keep her time alone with them as short as possible. I stopped short of screaming that I was their mother and she'd better not think that she was getting to take over any part of my job.

Despite my misgivings and in a relatively short space of time, I found I relaxed with the idea of a Chinese *ayi*. In a matter of weeks Tina became like an extra member of our family. I had gone from running around and cleaning up before she arrived and lingering longer than I should to make sure the kids were happy, to feeling very confident having Tina in the house and in charge of the children for the period Smarty and I were at work. She made an enormous difference to our daily lives in Shanghai, even if it was just removing a little of the daily stress. It was surprising how quickly we were able to adjust and become dependent on some elements of a new lifestyle.

Tina had only a tiny amount of English, but was very patient and happy to watch while I mimed directions. If our communication system faltered, she took notes home for translation by her fourteen-year-old daughter who studied English at school. We had developed our own routine. Tina cleaned while I put the children to sleep for an afternoon nap, and while I sneaked off to the bedroom to curl up with a book or go to the gym for an hour before I had to get ready for work. She could sew and mend whatever we managed to break. She could get things fixed because making S-bend gestures at the phone just didn't work with Chinese plumbers. She could grab shopping bags and hold little hands as I struggled to dodge the crazy traffic and hail a taxi after a trip to the store with both children in tow. She could read our bills and tell us when they were overdue and when we were about to get our power cut off. She could find a giant bag of wooden skewers for just a few yuan so I could make kebabs after I'd been looking for weeks and was prepared to start whittling the nearest flame tree. She made the best Chinese food we had tasted in Shanghai and she hovered while I cooked dinner for the children before I left for work, learning the dishes I prepared, chopping and slicing ingredients, and cleaning up as I went. As soon as the kids woke up in the afternoon, she whipped up snacks and drinks, waited while I had a play with them and said goodbye, then she'd whisk them off to have fun, either on their bikes, in the playground, or visiting their friends in other apartments in our compound. The kids adored her and were rarely disappointed when I explained that it was time for me to go to work and that they would have to stay with Tina. Both Milly and Nelson kept asking if Tina could come and play on weekends too.

From Tina's perspective, I may have become too comfortable having her around. I was standing at the kitchen sink washing up, naked to cool down after showering following a gym session. It was hours before Tina's regular starting time, but she came in unexpectedly to pop some treats for the kids in the fridge. Our eyes met as I darted into the laundry and started fishing about in the washing machine for something to cover myself. I'm not sure who was more taken aback and uncomfortable.

At the playgroup I attended with the kids I told a group of expat friends my embarrassing story in a discussion that had started on how to deal with *ayi*. We got on to the Chinese culture of domestic help and how we should treat our employees. I was feeling a little awkward and all a bit la-di-da nattering about the 'help'. I told my little anecdote about getting caught naked at the sink in the hope it would steer the conversation away from the whining of the privileged class. I was expecting quite a laugh. Rather I got quizzical looks.

The woman who had been living in China the longest piped up: 'And why were you washing up?'

In our complex there were many young children and as many *ayi*. I noticed that the *ayi* banded together so there was an informal kids club gathering most mornings and afternoons. I figured the *ayi* were making the best of the situation as well as giving the kids a bit of social interaction. Occasionally I headed down to the clubhouse mid-morning to find groups of *ayi* engaged in a ping-pong competition. I watched while the *ayi* fought it out for ping-pong supremacy while babies of all ages and nationalities clambered around underneath the tables or outside in the halls under the watchful eye of the *ayi* warming up for their shot at the table. When they were not playing ping-pong, many *ayi* took turns walking backwards around the One Park Avenue gardens – a trick many Chinese seemed keen to master. And they seemed to spend a lot of their time slapping different parts of their body, which was also a Chinese habit that was presumably carried out to boost circulation.

It had to be a peculiar, yet interesting upbringing for the expat child or Chinese baby of working parents. *Ayi*, in general, jumped to the demands of a child. In a society where children are so treasured, discipline was minimal and a child need only open its mouth and an *ayi* was there offering food from a chopstick or toothpick, wiping away any spill and watching intently to see when they could offer another tasty morsel or tend to the child's needs. Chinese children don't wear nappies so *ayi* were not accustomed to diapering children. I had kept Nelson in nappies when we went out so we could avoid the public squat toilets. For all Tina's qualifications, I couldn't convince her to put his nappy on tight enough to stop it falling down to his knees when he walked. Chinese children are generally toilet trained within months of birth. They wear split-back pants, leaving their little brown bottoms totally exposed and ready for action, which I initially thought was very cute but a little severe in winter. I was told that by the time Chinese children are eight months old, they can usually wee to the command of an *ayi* whistle, which avoids all sorts of messy toilet emergencies. I told my mother friends that when I worked for a while writing about the local horse races in Cairns in Australia's far north, I met a horse whistler whose job was to coax a urine sample from the horses for vet and drug tests after races. I suggested they inform their *ayi* that they may wish to branch out should horse racing, banned on the Chinese mainland since 1949, ever be permitted again and their nannying work dry up.

One of the greatest benefits for the expat child in having an *ayi* is the bilingual nature of their upbringing. I was very keen for Tina to only speak to the kids in Mandarin to help them develop their language skills. Both Milly and Nelson quickly developed some wonderful friendships with other children, but I was acutely aware that my kids were often the only single-language speakers. Milly had two best friends – one was a little girl called Nicole who had an Italian mother and Swedish father. She spoke both parent languages as well as Chinese and English. Milly's other close friend Victoria also spoke Chinese, English and Swedish. A pal of mine was fluent in six languages and her two children were gradually working up to their third. When groups of children like these got together it was not uncommon to hear them switching from English to Chinese, as well as Russian, Italian, Swedish and Spanish. When the common language in a group was Chinese rather than English it was my kids who felt a bit left out.

Multi- and bilingualism is a big deal in Shanghai. Chinese are learning English and expats are learning Chinese. Director of the Western International School of Shanghai, Dr Alfonso Orsini told *Shanghai Parents and Kids* magazine that the melting pot of Shanghai is a terrific breeding ground for multilingual children. He said a child's lack of inhibition allows them to absorb a language holistically, which is very important in learning Chinese. 'Speaking a language isn't just learning the grammar,' said Orsini. 'It's adopting the manner and mindset of the language.'

We were thankful children are so adept at absorbing languages when we headed out one night to our favourite Uighur-cuisine restaurant for dinner with friends. After about 90 minutes of waiting, one of the dishes we had ordered had still failed to arrive. It was the prawns, which was the kids' favourite. They were getting very hungry and starting to decide an increasingly raucous game of hide and seek might be preferable to sitting up to eat dinner at all. I had tried numerous times to explain to the waiters that the kids were famished and could they please ensure the dish arrived soon. Smarty had tried as well, as had the couple with whom we were dining. We thought their efforts may have achieved results as they had a far greater grasp of the language than we did. Eventually in despair, we resorted to taking the best Chinese speaker among us to deal with the situation. We briefed their three-year-old daughter Lucy on the reasons behind the absence of her dinner, took her down to the kitchen and waited while the gorgeous little Australian girl berated the kitchen staff in

Chinese for not getting her prawns to the table on time. The dish soon arrived.

Smarty and I were gradually picking up some of the language, but not nearly at the pace the children were. Tina and Nelson had their own secret little chats that he then had to interpret (mainly telling us he was refusing to clean his teeth as Tina had asked him to do). Milly, however, explained that she preferred to speak English because she didn't really like the sound of Chinese. I accepted her choice and her reasons and hoped that she was taking in far more than she realised. I did, however, notice that Tina's English was improving at a faster rate than Milly's Mandarin.

Smarty had developed quite the repertoire for ordering in Chinese. It came from his lunchtime visits to local restaurants with office colleagues. I was limited to taxi Chinese. With my street name pronunciations improving, I had been having fewer disasters and had started to get comfortable directing drivers to take left or right turns rather than sitting back hoping I had not been taken on a massive detour to get to my destination.

While I was quite pleased at my ability to communicate directions, my Chinese language skills in other areas remained appalling. So I resorted to the foreign language equivalent of that sometimes-handy, but usually annoying tool for speedy SMS senders: predictive text. Faced with a potential conversation in Chinese that didn't involve telling a taxi driver how to get home, I immediately leapt to assumptions, just like the texting option. With two children scampering around, I most often assumed I was being asked about the kids. I also considered myself on safe ground assuming that query involved: a) What are their names? b) How old are they? or c) is the small one with the long blond hair dressed in blue, roaring like a lion and carrying a truck, a boy or a girl?

My regular response had been to opt for option c and reply 'boy', while waving a little finger in what I considered a helpful gesture in bridging the language barrier. Alas, it had not been so helpful to my children, particularly Nelson. The moment I realised I needed to change tack occurred when, happily indulging in what I considered a cross-cultural exchange with a friendly *ayi* in the One Park foyer, Nelson looked at me quite quizzically, shook his head and uttered disapprovingly: 'No, Mum.' I was standing there foolishly, little finger cocked and saying 'boy', as he turned to the woman, addressed her in Mandarin, told her his name and proceeded to nod as she burst forth in conversation.

I was left hoping she wasn't telling him that his mother's ability to cause him great social discomfort was only going to get worse. It would mean my son would no longer consider me clever, cool and in control and that I had, in fact, turned into that most awful of creatures – the 'embarrassing mother'. It was while I stood on the outside of this bizarre Chinese exchange involving my little boy that memories of my horror at my own mother's behaviour came flooding back. I remembered her taking me downtown for the grand purchase of my first bra. And I still recalled her standing there, me turning crimson, as she asked the fitter if they had any bras to accommodate breasts the size of a fingernail. Seared into my mind was that as she did, she added the same gesture I had adopted in talking about Nelson – she was waving her littlest finger.

CHAPTER 11

A CLASS OF OUR OWN

Foreigners from all over the world have converged on Shanghai. The city's expat career centre said about 80 per cent of the 68 600 expats working in the city were from Japan, the United States, South Korea, Singapore, Germany, France, Canada, Malaysia, Australia and the United Kingdom. Many were senior company executives, with investors, board chairmen, general managers, chief representatives and partners making up about 32 per cent of the total of the foreign businesspeople who had made China's business hub their home.

There were huge perks for those on the big expat packages offered to executives and their families to come to China which had been experiencing a boom in trade and development. But the exec was also expected to work long hours and was often away from home. The person left to make a home for the family in Shanghai was called the 'trailing spouse'. The trailing spouse rarely had permission to work in China but got the spoils of the package such as a huge housing allowance, affording the family a villa lifestyle in the suburbs, education allowances for the children's private schooling, a car with a driver, at least one *ayi*, and any other help they deem necessary. Many trailing spouses found, relieved of domestic chores, they had unexpected time on their massaged and manicured hands. Identical navy Buick minivans were often lined up outside favourite expat haunts like the fabric markets, the pearl market or Western-food restaurants. It was a sure giveaway that there was an expat function nearby or the ladies were out to lunch.

There's only so much shopping anyone can do, even in Shanghai. An incredible number of the foreign women I met, many of whom were trailing spouses, had decided that they were never again going to be in a situation where they could afford so much help, so were taking the chance to have more babies. In a moment of joy and contentment at our new life in Shanghai, I even considered having another baby. The notion only lasted until Smarty asked if I'd gone completely mad. While we were both ridiculously enraptured with our two children and were fascinated to watch them emerging as little people in their own right, both of us had come to accept that I'm no fun when I'm pregnant and neither of us were really that into baby-derived sleeplessness.

Of the trailing spouses similarly disinclined to have babies whom I met at kindy, playgroup and foreigner networks in Shanghai during my free days, many told me they were filling their time by becoming skilled at mah-jong or taking on a mountain of volunteer work. I had been asked to join a number of volunteer organisations, including a club of expat women who knitted and donated their creations to Chinese children. I had to pass on the knitting. I wasn't sure even the most desperate child would appreciate my knitwear. Fortunately I was able to offer the excuse that I worked full-time.

Our life was significantly different to that of many other expats. We didn't have all the benefits of a spacious villa, slick new cars, loads of spare time and cash to burn. We'd been quite resistant to having anyone take over our parenting tasks so hadn't been able to experience a lot of the benefits of having an on-call child minder – such as sampling all the top-end restaurants, bars and nightlife in vibrant Shanghai. However, even though we both worked at different ends of the day, we did have time with each other. And we were living a shared experience, rather than having one person trying to forge a family life in a foreign environment while the other was navigating the pitfalls of doing business in China.

We soon realised that regardless of the package any expat is on, we all had one thing in common. No expat was immune to culture shock. Vicci Henderson, a counsellor and fifteen-year veteran of living the expat lifestyle in China, says in a helpful survival guide for expat families, *Shanghai for Kids*, that the influence of culture in daily life is not often appreciated until a person relocates. She says suddenly all your communication cues – body language, words, facial expressions, tone of voice, idioms and slang – no longer work. It makes daily tasks like catching a taxi and shopping hard. She says each interaction can put a chink in someone's confidence until the day ends with you a dishevelled, weepy mess struggling to understand why the Chinese directions you uttered in the morning were perfectly understood and ensured you were delivered to your child's kindergarten on time, but the same words in the afternoon resulted in you being sped across the river to other side of the city, only for it to take more than an hour, lots of distress and shouting and banging on the driver's protective capsule to get you back. (That last bit was me, not Mrs Henderson.)

The expats we had met, regardless of income or circumstance, told us they had all experienced similar highs and lows of the lifestyle. In a society that is fast and pushy and busy and brittle, many trailing spouses said it could be just as alienating and confronting to suddenly find yourself without purpose, with children taken care of, house cleaned and no job to do as it was to struggle through the day with children or a high-powered career to attend to. As a mother of two young children, I tapped into the support groups available in the city and gravitated towards expat women in a similar situation. I was a little unusual in that I lived the life of the primary child-carer and family organiser in a foreign land by day, and the money-earner, dealing with a Chinese workplace by night. But I was far from the only expat mum who bombarded support groups with questions. I was also not the only one who used them to help me keep my sanity after a particularly trying 'China day'. Such groups, whether they were informal like the playgroup mums at Koala Kids or members of the more organised Internet groups such as Shanghai Expat or Shanghai Mamas, were also very helpful in ensuring we had a place to vent our frustrations and keep perspective on our place as foreign guests in China.

The trailing spouse or the expat mum, from all the different strata of expat circumstances, had emerged as a strong and growing presence in Shanghai. We numbered in the thousands. We employed scores of local Chinese – while *ayi* are predominantly women, drivers are usually men – and we were relatively big local spenders. Women with time to shop were some of the bigger contributors to the local economy. These were the women who divided their time between the South Bund Fabric Market on Lujiabang Lu, which started as a sprawling street fair back in the early 1990s and was now three levels of fabric-filled stalls with tailors able to make or copy any design or outfit imaginable. The women also frequented Pearl City in Hongqiao, which sold jewellery as well as clothing and handbags, and the Knock-Off market on Nanjing Lu, another multi-level hall of vendors selling designer-copy clothing, handbags and shoes. There were also flower markets, electronics markets, hidden markets and food markets. And that's before the women hit the actual shops. Expats in general contributed to the local economy by paying inflated 'non Chinese' prices even for groceries (who else would pay 74.90 yuan (A$12) for a box of Cheerios, 51.30 yuan ($8.30) for a box of Coco Pops or about $15 for a bag of Doritos?). Expat mothers also forked out the expensive fees of about A$30 a lesson charged for children's enrichment activities like music classes, painting classes and dancing. The classes in which a little English was spoken were the most expensive, and they were always full.

China is a society that loves to define people according to class. But I found so many of the expat mums in Shanghai didn't fit the class label most often assigned to us. While some might fit the bill, most of my expat friends and acquaintances were not 'tai tai' – a privileged woman of boundless money and spare time who could win a gold medal for shopping. I started thinking that with so many of us living in Shanghai, and becoming a legitimate element of the society, there should be a label that suited us. To save exhaustively reading sociological texts on the issue of class, I delved into some Chinese chick lit for a cure to my sense of labellessness.

In Annie Wang's *People's Republic of Desire*, there was a little bite among the racy exploits of the lead character and her girlfriends that contained an analysis of social class in modern Chinese cities. Wang was part of a new wave of young female Chinese writers producing Chinese urban novels. Along with writers like Wei Hui, whose rather morose novel *Shanghai Baby* had been turned into a feature film, these women were considered the young female voice of new China. Class is just not something that we really talk about openly in Australia, but is done explicitly in China where people are candidly classified as white collars, blue collars and peasants. Peasants are the poorest class and are mostly farmers.

There had been a mass influx of peasants to Shanghai looking for work, which had prompted quite a backlash from the Shanghainese who thought these migrant workers had brought crime and trouble to the city. The government, fearing the rush to the cities meant the nation would not have enough people working the land to feed itself, had begun a new round of boosting the status of peasants, farming and agriculture in China. This was why, officially, there were no poor connotations associated with calling someone a peasant in China. Due to my own sensibilities, however, I still found it jarring when one of my colleagues told me a story about his grandmother the peasant.

In her novel, Wang devoted a chapter to the breakdown of classes in new China, especially as they related to women. She described the *xiaozi*, or petit bourgeois. To have been called *xiaozi* was apparently dangerous during the Cultural Revolution, although not as dangerous as being called counter-revolutionary, and meant one had committed offences against the People's Fashion such as wearing high heels or permed hair. Wang wrote that being called *xiaozi* was now extremely cool and involved reading Chinese versions of *Elle* and *Cosmopolitan* and drinking coffee instead of tea.

The new elite, *xingui*, were also cool. And they were rich. They read *Fortune* magazine or *Business Week*, they drove BMWs, took lovers, and attended banquets every week. *Xingui* were often the children of the Shanghai or Beijing upper class who were afforded a Western education and worked for multinational banks or Fortune 500 companies.

Wang also described the bobos, bourgeois bohemians. They were the SUV-driving, *Time*-magazine-reading, world-travelling vegetarians who had iPods full of new age music and did yoga. Wang said bobos also had more than fifteen years education and tended to sleep under down quilts.

Women in China have not had an easy run of it, with girls generally only getting a shot at education, a career and independence since 1949. At that time, under a slogan of the era that said, 'Women hold up half the sky,' daughters, wives and mothers were encouraged to learn how to read and write and contribute in the workforce. In this period they were able to go to school, start university, or get a job in a factory. Jean Wu, the CEO of China Helpline, a phone-based translation service in Shanghai, said she went to school during this time. She said she was placed into a kindergarten aged two and only came home on Sundays. She said her parents ate in a public kitchen, set up to free women from household chores, so her father and her mother had more time to work. Wu said women were encouraged to work and pursue a career as much as the men, but these new opportunities for women also meant they faced the same denunciations as men during the Cultural Revolution.

These days, women still push to work as hard and as long as men, primarily to raise enough money to give their child every chance at advancement in China's super competitive education system. However, women in China are again experiencing the brunt of change. In China, despite being as qualified as men, women are losing their equality at the entry level in the workplace. With the global financial crisis, a growing number of recruiting ads in Shanghai state 'male only' applicants for the positions as employers who are looking to tighten their budgets don't want women who are going to leave the workforce to have a child.

Many of the expat women I met were not only highly educated but had left good jobs behind to come and not work in China. It seemed the volunteer associations and clubs in Shanghai had been the main beneficiaries of all this talent. I thought many of these women were adventurous and remarkable and wanted to contribute to the society in which they were making their home. And, because it was important in China to be classed and categorised, I thought we deserved a label that went beyond being a foreigner or being a mother and reflected the positives of the expat women in Shanghai.

It was exciting to be part of a community that included people from so many different backgrounds and who had so many reasons for being in China. While many of our friends had arrived courtesy of a company posting, many others had arrived on their own dollar to pursue their own economic opportunities. Still others had chosen China for a lifestyle they felt they could not afford at home and the safe environment it offered their children. Through our normal daily activities we developed a social circle that included a high level businessman who was longing for a surf, an Australian and her Japanese executive husband who played in a Beatles tribute band, a gregarious Swede, sassy New Yorkers, and fashionable Italians who managed to source the most amazing imported cheese, as well as local Shanghainese, Hong Kong and mainland Chinese.

It was a peculiarly Shanghai expat way of life. We were all starting to quite enjoy it. Strangely, China and the big city we found ourselves in had almost begun to feel like home. I'd become accustomed to the noise, the smell, the grey. I could cross the road confidently, predicting where the cyclists would part, where the cars would stop or turn, and when the horns were beeping for danger or for fun. I liked that under a murky sky, the Huangpu River looked just as dirty brown as it did on a clear day and that there was no let up in the procession of green barges of coal that slid low-down in the water like crocodiles slipping through the city. I was no longer so dazzled by the fanciful buildings shooting towards the clouds, but rather accepted the pointy steel and glass towers that looked like pineapples and rocket ships and amusement rides as part of my city's skyline. I was accustomed to getting a smile out of the brightly coloured kites that fluttered against the cloudy haze as I headed into People's Square near the river. And I felt comfortable spending an hour bargaining and browsing through all the toys, trinkets and clothes at the Pu'an Lu children's market, even though I really only needed to pop in to pick up a new pair of shoes for the kids.

I didn't doubt for a minute the statistic I had been told that about one quarter of the world's cranes were working in Shanghai. They were spotted around the city like coconut on a lamington. There was seemingly not a city block that didn't contain a demolition or a building site. Great piles of bamboo scaffolding rose like pick-up-sticks to the highest levels of new buildings. Bamboo is in the middle of a revival in China, and apparently throughout the architectural world. It's being called 'vegetal steel', it's lighter than steel but five times stronger than concrete. I liked that I knew this detail about my urban landscape, but remained wary of the hollow grass constructions as I had to walk under at least three sets of scaffolding every day.

I had started to form mini-friendships with the people I saw daily. The fruit shop woman had been teaching me to say numbers in Chinese and would patiently wait while I attempted to extract the correct money for her without having to resort to the calculator to check I understood our transaction. I was getting bolder at wandering down laneways and alleys and peeking into doorways without feeling like I was imposing on people's privacy. I had a favourite clothing store where the woman would rush out into the street to grab me on my way past if she had any new items that might come in my size. I bought only one cashmere swing jacket from her in an entire year, yet managed to spend an enormous amount of time in her store, chatting about fabric and style – I think. I tried to buy shoes, too, from roadside stores, yet found I was afflicted with 'man feet' when it came to dainty Chinese shoe sizes. I caused much amusement attempting to try on the latest styles, but not as much as when I actually had to wear Smarty's shoes down to the store because the zip on my own boots had broken. The laughing started the minute I walked into the shop to buy a replacement pair of boots. After seeing my makeshift size 10 men's footwear they ushered me straight back out the door with a shake of the head.

I had become more accustomed to not fitting in, but was starting to feel like I could make it through each day. And then I made my grand mistake. I got cocky.

I blame it all on taxis. It all started when I was heading home from the Singing Speckled Frogs at the Ambassy Club on Huahai Lu with Nelson – one of the activities I indulged in to amuse my son as well as to try to forge bonds with other expat mums and their kids. Nelson ultimately proved uninterested in the nursery rhyme singing, preferring to eat biscuits and steal the other children's musical instruments, which left me to sing on my own and look on while the well-behaved Chinese children did as they were told and *ayi* chased their expat charges around the room.

On leaving, I hailed a taxi and explained in my best Mandarin precisely where I wanted to go. With the smugness that comes with finding your feet in a new city, I was feeling terribly in control as I directed the taxi driver home to Xinzha Lu. I realised I still had to organise something for dinner and asked my cab driver to pull over a block from home so I could whip down to the one shop that I knew had spaghetti and canned tuna in stock. The car stopped. I paid, gathered bags and Nelson together and opened the car door. Unfortunately, I didn't check precisely where we had pulled up. The driver had stopped right in the middle of the road. With my open door, I managed to collect a man riding his motorbike past on the inside lane. He hurtled over the cab door, leaving his bike behind, which then collected another motorbike rider, and, for good measure, a couple of cyclists. It was bedlam. A massive crowd gathered. I was pulled out of the back of the taxi. The poor bloke on the road was hauled to his feet and ordered by all to display his wounds – like I didn't feel bad enough. Then the taxi driver began berating me, the crowd started berating me (it was all in Chinese, but didn't sound at all sympathetic). Others started yelling into their phones, which I soon realised were calls to the police. Meanwhile, the motorbike rider was bleeding, the crumpled bikes were being wheeled off to the side of the road and I was stuck. My morning confidence evaporated. I adopted my only possible recourse. I clutched on to Nelson and started crying.

The police arrived and everyone started yelling again. I seriously thought about doing a runner, but figured I might be easy to spot. The officer headed over to me, where I was still sniffling and trying to look as innocent as possible. He leaned down and said in English: 'Where are you from?'. I told him Australia, to which he replied: 'Ah, Odaliya. Yes, very nice'. Then he walked off, got on his bike and rode away.

I was somewhat cheered, but the police officer's ambivalence to the chaos I had caused did not appease the crowd. They started pulling money out and waving it at me in gestures that meant I had to pay. They demanded I pay the taxi driver for the damage and the motorbike rider for his injuries. I considered inspecting his injuries because, from where I stood, it looked only like a bit of a scratch on the knee now that the bleeding had subsided. But I didn't think it was the wisest course. I had no option if I was to escape the mob. I threw 300 yuan ($A48.90), which was all I was carrying, and fled. It was street justice, Shanghai-style.

With all the drama, it had taken me about an hour to finally get home. I realised it was just about time to go back and pick Milly up from kindy. It meant I had to take another taxi.

CHAPTER 12

BEHIND THE FACADE

I discovered a new park. It was less than a block from our home. Bird chirping had been greeting us most mornings as the cold of winter eased into spring, yet the source of the trilling, utterly incongruous with the normal morning cacophony of horns blasting, engines revving, bellowing and barking, eluded me. To this point, I'd failed to find anything birdlike flying around Shanghai other than the hardy sparrows that often make cities their home. Yet I'd suddenly found birds. They sat in a little patch of green, in cages hanging from just about every tree in a park where people brought their prized pet song thrushes to sing while they sat and smoked and chatted and listened among the greenery and the twitters of their surrounds. And I didn't know about it at all. There was a whole park at the end of an alley, off a main street and behind a local hospital literally metres from our apartment. It was hidden, a mystery. Until then.

It had been like that since our arrival in Shanghai. We might take the same walk every day, yet occasionally, with a change of pace or a glance down a different alley, up would pop an incredible surprise. We couldn't believe how much there was – and how much we had missed – behind the street facades, even within a couple of blocks of our home. So we made it a project to pull back the covers on Shanghai – or at least take a little more time to find out what was going on in our neighbourhood.

I'd begun noticing, and for some reason counting, the number of times the flowers were changed in the gardens at the entrance to our residential complex. (It was nine times in five months.) The more-often-than-not mixture of colourful pansies was rarely watered, instead they were dug up and new flowers planted every few weeks. It became an unofficial starting point for me on my daily walk to work: have the pansies been changed? Will the tulips that made an altogether-too-brief appearance make their return? What will I see that's different today?

I saw that while the pansies might not be watered, the bare footpath was. Saving the environment, conservation and recycling were concepts that were just taking hold in Shanghai, but there was little attempt to save water with all the concrete hosing that took place. There must have been an arbitrary groove in the sidewalk near one of the city's upmarket plazas that defined the point at which cleaners were instructed by authorities to begin polishing each night.

They used chemicals that wore out the soles of your boots then scrubbers and hoses that pumped out great streams of water which all went down the nearest drain.

The cleanest block would have to be the one surrounding Plaza 66 that fronts Nanjing Lu. Plaza 66 is home to exclusive stores such as Tiffany's, Prada, Christian Dior and Louis Vuitton. I couldn't help but think of a Chinese acquaintance every time I walked past the shimmering, freshly scrubbed towers. She seemed to sum up the mad consumerism that had taken hold in Shanghai. We were lazing by the pool at the Portman Ritz-Carlton complex down from Plaza 66 on Nanjing Lu while the children had a swim. She was telling me about her little boy. I asked his name. 'As soon as I saw he was a boy, I knew I had to name him after my favourite handbag' she said. 'His name is Louis, after Louis Vuitton.' I'm not sure my fake oversize Prada sunglasses covered my surprise.

Plaza 66 was not far from one of my favourite hole-in-the-wall eateries, ranked by name if not for its offerings. It was called 'Delicious Gruel' at the corner of Xikang and Beijing Xie roads. I was usually drawn away from the tiny café, however, by the aroma of outlets a little further down Xikang Lu that were always doing a brisk business in the warmer weather. One sold noodles and the other made on-the-spot rustic pancake/roti concoctions with meat and vegetable fillings. There was always a crowd and I kept stopping and watching and trying to identify the ingredients, which must have been a tad annoying for the owner. I hadn't actually eaten there as I often saw them adding water to their batch of pancake mix from a tap on the footpath and the cook mixing it with his bare hands while sitting out next to the street where I feared there was a good chance cars and buses could splash all sorts of gunk into the batter.

Nearby we had a few niche services. On my daily walk, I could now acknowledge our three local key-cutters, two bag repairers, a shoe-repairer, a bicycle repairer, and someone on Shaanxi Bei Lu who either wanted to sell me a sewing machine or take up my trouser hems. I felt like such a local. I also knew to dodge a particular corner on Nanjing Lu due to an overzealous shoe-shiner who even tried to polish sneakers. One day he wasn't in his usual spot to catch the passing tourists – it appeared he was muscled out by a hustler with a pet monkey.

If I walked from our apartment away from Nanjing Lu, I found Wuding Lu, a street that had become one of my favourites for it retained pockets that were far from gentrified. Directly behind One Park Avenue was a run-down old local housing area in the throes of being consumed by modern apartments. One Park Avenue's sister complex, Eight Park Avenue, had begun gobbling up the maze of alleys and ramshackle old houses beside it. Back behind the street fronts where people were cooking vegetables and boiling water in shelters made of wood and wrought iron was a scar that was being prepared for the construction of a new tennis court or swimming pool. On Wuding Lu, I had found a fish shop with great tubs of fish and prawns, frogs and sometimes turtles. It was not a pet shop as I originally thought. There was also a butcher that stacked cuts of meat on boards out on the street. There were fruit and vegetable shops and, in the middle of it all, a foot massage parlour, a bike repair stall that spilled out across the footpath and onto the street, and an Avon outlet. The area looked like a slum compared with residential towers like One Park Avenue, but it was always busy and full of life with the smell of freshly cooked food flowing from the numerous kitchens, along with the hum of conversation from the residents who sat in the gutters or on the footpaths on dilapidated old couches and rickety chairs.

To broaden our view of the neighbourhood, I had taken to Smarty's trick of getting around town. He called it following the green man. Under the rules of this game, there was to be no loitering at street corners waiting to cross. Rather, whichever direction showed a green light for crossing the street, then that was the path that was taken. I hadn't ended up much more than 30 minutes late for work following this pattern. But it had taken me into alleys and nooks I had previously ignored and it was how I discovered possibly the only local stockist of cheap shoes that would fit my feet on Wuding Lu. It was how I stumbled upon the 'Pick-A-Boo' Hairdressers down on an alley on Nanjing Lu and passed 'Sooth Wind Massage' on a stroll down Fuxing Lu. It was how I came to find a fabulous local market on Yu Yuan Lu with leather jackets, baseball shirts, sunglasses and handbags. I was so impressed, I brought Smarty back a week later. The market had been demolished.

There were three schools and a university within three blocks of our apartment. It was only the crowd of parents and school kids in uniform every afternoon that gave the school's location away. Otherwise the schools were hidden behind big iron gates and looked like a row of empty shops. The local hospitals, however, didn't disguise their presence, opting instead for literal signage that contained English translations. One block away from where we lived was the Diarrhoea Hospital. It was right near the Plastic and Laser

Surgery Hospital, and the pictures of babies and toys turned out to be a giveaway about the Children's Hospital. Away from the hospital zone, Xinzha Lu turned into a bicycle repair and hardware street. Heading towards the river, store after store selling bicycles tubes, wheels, chains, locks and repair kits, sat side by side.

We had taken to following the green man on walks at the weekend to see where we'd end up, but could only take the stroller with Nelson strapped in so far before we'd trip over potholes, bicycles, piles of rubble, chairs and people selling vegetables and other wares. Shanghai is tough terrain for the pram-bound. Even after strolling past the very upmarket Chartres Restaurant on the corner of Fuxing and Huashan roads, Nelson and I suddenly found ourselves ploughing through a building site that had sprung up beside the fancy-looking restaurant. We got stuck in mounds of rubble and scattered bicycle wheels and wheelbarrows. There was washing hanging out to dry on lines strung to trees and a lamppost. And there were workers sitting on piles of rubbish eating dumplings.

On Beijing Lu, a street where hundreds of shops sold electronic parts, we wandered past pockets of early style *lilong*. They were still very much lived in, with No. 803 Beijing Lu a typical picture of Shanghai domestic life featuring clothes strung up to dry, people sitting and chatting or smoking or cooking or wandering around in their pyjamas. *Lilong* are generally fronted by commercial shopfronts with the residential compounds behind. A primary lane runs through the *lilong* around which the homes are clustered in rows on smaller secondary lanes that run at right angles to the main laneway. It was, and remains, a very crowded lifestyle. The urban development of Shanghai may have swept away much of the old landscape, but there have been efforts to retain some elements of the old lifestyle. *Lilong* life included a communal well (*jing*) and coal stoves (*meiqiulu*). The smell of the coal stoves firing up was, for many, the familiar scent of a new dawn. The *Shanghai Daily* unearthed a terrific story about a water-pipe tree that was being moved to a museum after the local community block at 63 Chang'an Road by Suzhou Creek was slated for 'urban reconstruction'. The rezoning meant everybody was to be booted out of their homes, the buildings demolished, and brand new structures put in place. The water tree was more than 50 years old and the only water pipeline tree still standing in the city. It came about because residents got tired of accessing only one tap in the courtyard to wash rice, vegetables and clothes, so they grafted tubes onto the water main and directed some of the flow to their own residences. The result was a jumbled, multi-coloured 'water-pipe tree' with the main 'trunk' line and 'branches' darting off in all directions – highly practical, utterly unsightly, but well worth a look for an insight into locals' daily lives.

One of the most typical sights in old laneways, and which still remains an obsession of sorts among the Chinese today, are chamber pots (*matong*). The pots are made with wooden pieces connected with bronze or iron and painted red or black. There is apparently an old Shanghai saying: 'New chamber pot smells good in the first three days.' Chamber pots feature prominently in Chinese sayings and in traditions. I was told that when a couple is married, it is one of the obligations of the family of the bride to prepare a new chamber pot as part of the bride's dowry (*jiazhuang*). On the day of the wedding, the chamber pot is carried amid much pomp into the bridegroom's home by one of the males of the bride's family. When taken into the newlywed's home it is filled with Chinese dates, lotus, peanuts and dried longan pulp (a popular fruit in Shanghai that looks like an eyeball and tastes a bit like a lychee). The mixture in the pot (*zao sheng gui zi*) means 'having a baby soon'. Emptying and cleaning chamber pots – commonly used throughout the city until the late 1980s – was a very important task. A cleaner would come through the neighbourhood early each morning with a big wooden cart to empty the chamber pots placed outside the homes in the laneways. The cleaner was euphemistically called the 'night soil' collector. The night soil was carted to the outskirts of the city and used by farmers on their crops. The practice may have been replaced by plumbing about 30 years ago, but we still continued to scrub and soak anything that we couldn't peel or boil before eating.

The produce being sold out on the street in most Shanghai neighbourhoods looked fantastic. I loved walking along Wulu-muqi Lu where there were vendors selling all sorts of dumplings, frogs, crabs, chestnuts, fish, vegetables, and huge pots of dried, crackly mystery ingredients that might be from the river or sea. It was messy and it was noisy. There were always people lined up at a few of the dumpling shops while sour-looking cooks at the almost-empty dumpling stores next door looked on. There were vendors balancing polystyrene containers of fish on their bicycles. There were cuts of meat sitting out for sale on cutting boards. On one occasion, a man even pulled up next to me on his bike and offered to sell me a recently deceased chicken.

Some streets throughout the city are famous for their local street food. We had taken a liking to Wujiang Lu which was small and sold great BBQ. It was a popular street, so there were plenty of people which meant pushing and shoving and elbows and trodden-on feet all became part of the process of getting dinner. The street's flagship store was Xiao Yang's Fried Dumplings (54 and 60 Wujiang Lu). There were also outlets offering grills of octopus and chicken and big fat spring rolls and fried tofu. There was a dense cloud of oil from all the frying and barbecuing going, and people wandering everywhere while cars and bicycles and motorbikes still gamely tried to drive through the maze of feasting locals.

Other streets kept their treasures better hidden. I had taken Milly to kindy every day for months and then walked about two blocks to take Nelson to playgroup or a music lesson at a residential compound nearby. It turned out that in the basement of a non-descript building that I had passed regularly on these walks was one of the world's best collections of Communist Party propaganda posters of the Mao Zedong era of 1949 to 1979. In the Shanghai Propaganda Poster Art Centre, a few hundred of a collection of more than 4000 original posters, are displayed. The posters are accompanied by startlingly direct commentary, which perhaps explains why the centre is in a basement secreted in a building set back off Huashan Lu. 'During the Cultural Revolution, artists had virtually no individual freedom of expression or hope of any material reward for their work,' according to the centre's Yang Pei Ming. 'They were instructed that art must serve politics. In order to meet the political demands made upon them, artists were obliged to produce iconic, inspirational works which effectively extolled the political messages promoted by the Party.' Yang Pei Ming said he hoped the 'nightmare' of the Cultural Revolution was never forgotten. He said he was preserving the posters 'cultivated by the tears and blood of people (that) have witnessed the happiness and bitterness of China.'

Among the collection I saw images of Chairman Mao as the red sun shining down on sunflowers symbolising the Chinese people. Depictions of the cheering masses, waving the little red book of quotations as a radiant Mao looks over them, were tagged with slogans 'Long Live the Victory of Mao Zedong Thought', 'Long Live the Great Leader, Teacher, Director and Helmsman Chairman Mao' and 'World is Bright All Over Once Follow Mao Zedong'. The posters, from 1966 when the Cultural Revolution began, support the relocation of students and intellectuals to the countryside and rail against America with slogans like: 'All World People Unite to Defeat US Imperialism and its Running Dogs'. During the height of the Cold War, posters between 1963 and 1965 carried slogans like 'US Imperialism Is the Common Enemy of The World', 'Heroic Women Militia' and images of peasant girls being presented with firearms by their proud mothers as their Red Army brothers look on under the slogan: 'Remember Class Hatred and Hold Tight Gun in Hand'.

In 1979, when Deng Xiaoping came to power, he abolished the 'big character poster' and propaganda posters. All propaganda materials were dumped from government organisations and sent to recycling factories. It is one of the reasons this out-of-the-way collection of posters is so remarkable. And why looking behind the modern facades can reveal so much more of the real China.

CHAPTER 13

IS THAT ELVIS
IN EMERGENCY?

We couldn't say we weren't warned. We'd been told right from the start that living in Shanghai would mean exposure to a whole new array of viruses and ailments and that we would all likely fall ill. We became regular visitors to our Chinese doctor. His office even started calling us to check on our wellbeing if we hadn't visited for a while.

It was only a few weeks into our Shanghai experience before we faced our first emergency. Milly developed a chronic cough which had us extremely concerned, but it was Nelson who woke in the freezing small hours of the morning with a raging temperature. We didn't know what to do other than cool him and administer the children's Panadol I'd thrown into the suitcase at the last minute. At that stage we didn't know where any hospitals were. We didn't know how to say 'hospital' to a taxi driver. We were so new to Shanghai, we didn't know anyone who could help, especially at such an hour. Bernie Leo had provided us with the business card of an English-speaking Chinese doctor. Thankfully, we'd kept it safe like a prized possession. Fraught with worry we watched the clock as we wiped Nelson down with chilled wash cloths and waited for 8 a.m. when we could, hopefully, reach someone at the doctor's surgery.

An assistant at the surgery answered our 8.01 a.m. phone call. We told her we were on the way in with a sick child, but were unsure if she understood. We piled in a taxi, presenting the doctor's business card written in Chinese and urged the driver to hurry. The doctor's surgery, Shanghai Comfort Medical Group St Reiss Medical Centre in the French Concession, fortunately was expecting us and founder and managing partner Dr Andrew Ngai was in.

St Reiss Medical Centre was a curious mix of Chinese and Western health care. As we walked into the surgery past the Chinese nurses and chemists, we saw a waiting area with English-language children's books, a bowl of lollies on the table, an AFL football and a cricket bat. On the wall were framed qualifications and thank-you letters for Dr Ngai's medical services. As I frantically filled in details of the children's immunisations, I looked up to see a face that I recognised on the wall leading to the four consulting rooms. Nelson pointed to the picture claiming he could see his grandfather, Pa. It wasn't Pa. It was Bob Hawke. In the photograph, the former Australian Prime Minister was sitting with his wife, Blanche d'Alpuget, and Dr Ngai. Underneath the photograph was a handwritten message. Heartened we were to be receiving medical care from the man chosen by the former PM when in China I read the letter.

Dear Andrew,

Thank you so much for your great skill and the care you gave Bob and me when we were in Shanghai … Your treatment made an enormous difference to us when we were ill: from utter misery, to optimism. Happily, I will not risk China again, except for Hainan (the Boao forum) and the Olympics, when the air should be cleaner than now. But do please be in touch if you come to Sydney.

With gratitude and best wishes,

Blanche d'Alpuget

I couldn't decide whether this made me feel better or not. I feared we were all doomed to suffer from China's ability to inflict sickness and misery.

Dr Ngai called us through. Immediately, he started wiping Nelson down with alcohol rub to open the blood vessels and allow the heat to escape my baby's small burning body. Nelson was diagnosed with acute tonsillitis and acute bronchitis. Dr Ngai took a look at Milly and she got the same diagnosis. The treatment, Dr Ngai said, had to start with an inter-muscular shot of antibiotics. Both children screamed through the giant needles that were plunged into their backsides. Smarty and I were both in shock and sick with worry that we had brought our precious children to such a city that made them so ill and caused such trauma. We were told we needed to bring the children back for the next three days for more needles and were prescribed four different medications for each child for the following two weeks. We left with a shopping bag full of drugs and two children so exhausted and stressed that they collapsed asleep in our arms. We wondered what the hell we had done.

We realised that what we did need was an emergency plan. Other mothers had told me horror stories of ambulances failing to turn up, how they had had their children misdiagnosed, been given overdoses or the wrong drugs and, in one terrible case, a mother and her son having to be airlifted to Singapore for treatment after things went so badly in Shanghai.

The health system sounded fractured, unreliable and complicated. There were hospitals that treated only specific illnesses like skin diseases, or cuts or broken bones. There were hospitals favoured by foreigners and there were special wings in local hospitals where you could get 'VIP' service, if you could pay. The system sounded even worse for locals. An expat who witnessed a traffic accident told us of having to take four victims in a taxi to the nearest hospital after an ambulance failed to turn up. Once there, the doctor asked him to register the victims who were complete strangers and pay a registration fee before they could be examined. He didn't have enough cash for all four so had to hand over his credit card. His advice was to remember to carry at least 2000 yuan in cash before getting injured in an accident.

I'd also been warned of the enormous reliance in China on antibiotic use. It had become such a problem and led to so many strains of antibiotic-resistant bugs that there had been a crackdown on doctors across the country handing out antibiotics. A national seminar in Shanghai on the 'Smart Use of Antibiotics' revealed that the antibiotic resistance rate reached as high as 80 per cent in China in 2001. The international level at the time was 30 per cent. It also reported the consumption of antibiotics accounted for 35 per cent of the total medical bills in Shanghai. Another study found that of the 1000 or so patients who showed up each day in 2004 with respiratory complaints at Shanghai's Children's Hospital, attached to the Fudan University, two-thirds were treated with antibiotics. The crackdown on antibiotic overuse, especially for children, occurred in 2006. Yet doctors were reporting that parents were still demanding more and stronger antibiotics for their sick children.

On top of antibiotics, people had also turned to intravenous drips, used extensively in China to replace lost fluids and considered by many as a panacea for most ills. The demand for the drips boiled over into violence in winter when so many people turned up for treatment at the Children's Hospital that parents of sick children launched a raid on the hospital pharmacy for medicine because they had been left waiting for hours to get their children on to intravenous drips. The *Shanghai Daily* reported the children were predominantly suffering colds and diarrhoea. After waiting up to five hours at the hospital, parents overwhelmed security guards to raid the pharmacy. The facility is the only city-based paediatric hospital in Minhang District and handles 4500 to 5000 outpatients every day. Some 800 to 900 children were being given saline drips each day, and another 500 at night. After the incident, officials extended outpatient hours and ordered doctors and nurses to work longer hours each day.

Our own health woes continued beyond winter. As the year progressed Nelson and Milly suffered recurring bouts of flu and bronchitis. Nelson was even diagnosed with pneumonia. We pumped enormous amounts of anti-cough and anti-fever medicine through them and every visit to the doctor ended with the children screaming, 'no needles in my bottom!'.

Smarty was also afflicted by recurrent bouts of respiratory illnesses and severe stomach upsets. He managed to avoid a lot of the antibiotic injections but was routinely hooked up to a drip. We began fearing there must be an underlying problem for the continued illnesses. At one of Smarty's visits to Dr Ngai for a stomach bug, he was told while attached to an intravenous drip, that there were visiting specialists available who could check him out to see if there were other issues causing him to repeatedly fall ill. Smarty agreed and was taken into another room where two sage and elderly-looking professors had agreed to run some tests.

The first specialist was a dermatologist. He checked Smarty's hands and feet, knees and back and declared he did not have eczema. Through the nurse who was acting as an interpreter, the specialist asked why Smarty was worried about his skin if his symptoms were stomach cramps and diarrhoea? Smarty offered no real answer. He had begun to think his day at the doctor's was going to be quite bizarre.

The second professor was a heart specialist. Through the nurse who was interpreting, she again took down a list of Smarty's symptoms. She said she was going to carry out an ECG, a recording of the electrical activity of the heart. To do this, she needed to attach some electrodes or electrical pulse monitors to Smarty's chest. He agreed to the test and reclined on the bench in the consulting room as the two female assistants attempted to attach the electrodes. The problem was, his chest was so hairy, the electrodes wouldn't stick. In stilted English, one of the assistants asked if she could shave patches of his chest so they could carry out the test. Smarty again agreed and, with a few giggles, the nurses fetched some disposable razors. They started shaving, but the razor soon clogged and refused to fell much of the hairy growth. Other assistants arrived to help. Soon there were five females attempting to shave Smarty's chest, still with limited success. Smarty decided that he'd best take matters into his own hands. He grabbed the razor, by now blunted from the previous pruning, and started shaving himself. The five assistants leaned in. Chinese males in general have less body hair than Caucasian males, so Smarty sensed he was a bit of an unusual specimen. He kept up the shave with the dulled blade, feeling a little like he was in the scene-setting stages of a low budget pornographic film. Finally the professor intervened. She abandoned the shaving show. And the ECG. She checked Smarty's pulse in his wrist and declared him just fine. He wandered back out to where I was waiting, with a strange look on his face and clumps of hair missing from all over his chest. I immediately went into a panic, thinking they must have found something awful like a cancerous growth and commenced chemotherapy or placed him on some sort of heavy duty antibiotic that had caused him to start shedding hair like a mangy dog. My concern, and sympathy, evaporated when he told me the real story.

In China, despite relatively limited living space, most master bedrooms in furnished expat compounds have a king-sized bed. With our children either in the early throes of a new illness or just recovering, it seemed they always ended up spending the night sleeping in our bed. Even with a spacious king-sized bed, it was a cosy arrangement. For Smarty in particular, it was a literal pain in the neck. After one particularly troublesome kids-in-the-bed night, he managed to wake with his head wedged between the bed and the bedside chest of drawers. Regular pain killers were not up to the task of relieving the injury. He decided he needed help. After his encounter with the medical specialists, he decided he would rather look for alternatives to our regular doctor.

Prior to coming to China, Smarty would have headed straight to his local physiotherapist for such an injury. However, he was told by work colleagues that in China, Traditional Chinese Medicine was a far better option. Traditional Chinese Medicine (TCM) is a system of preventing, diagnosing and curing disease that has been practised in China for about 5000 years. TCM has its origins in ancient Taoist philosophy, which views a person as an energy system in which body and mind are unified, each influencing and balancing the other. TCM emphasises a holistic approach that makes use of acupuncture, herbal medicine, massage and diet. Under TCM, it is taught that the human body comprises two opposing yet mutually dependent halves – Yin and Yang. When the balance is broken it causes blockages in the flow of qi (energy of life force) along the body's pathways or meridians. TCM believes in a close relation between the outside of the human body and the organs inside. The changes of vital energy, blood, and the Yin and Yang of internal organs are said to be reflected on the body surface. I got a quite a long lecture at one point by a Chinese colleague on just how much you can tell about a person's health and state of their internal organs by the colour of their tongue. It sounds quite the party trick.

I had not experienced TCM but noticed the side effects of one of the practices called cupping. I had seen quite a few people in Shanghai with large, red welts on their neck, back and shoulders. I had feared there must be a strange skin condition that left circular red and purple markings on the sufferer. Cupping therapy, *huo guan* (literally 'fire cupping') is a treatment that is said to relieve pain caused by blocked energy and blood. It is also used to treat indigestion, coughing and insomnia. The way it works is that a cup, about 5 centimetres in diameter, is applied to the skin. The pressure in the cup is reduced by heating, sometimes putting a piece of burning paper inside or by suctioning out the air. The vacuum draws the skin and muscle into the cup which is left in place for about 15 minutes. The heat and vacuum are said to draw out 'pathogenic' cold and damp – bad things upsetting the body's balance that are either causing disease or have the potential to do so. Cupping is usually applied to the back on acupuncture points or where pain is felt. The effects of the 'remedy' look terribly painful.

Food and herbal remedies are also a major part of TCM. Traditional Chinese Medicine holds that eating certain foods prepared in a certain way in a certain season is crucial for good health. In TCM, seasonings are not only for flavour, but for health. Bitter foods, for example, are said to aid the lungs, while spicy food builds Yang energy in the kidneys. Sweetness can apparently combat too much energy in the liver, sourness can help reduce excessive heat in the heart, and saltiness can help prevent overworking the spleen. But too much salty food will thicken the blood and undermine circulation and too much bitter food can make skin look old and the hair fall out. Too much spicy food causes tendons to lose elasticity, thick skin may get thicker if a person overdoes the sour food and too many sweets can cause achy bones and more hair loss.

The *Shanghai Daily* ran a weekly page on TCM. It explained eating was about retaining balance. People with too much internal heat should eat 'cold' foods while 'cold' people should eat 'hot' foods to rebalance energy. This was why in North China, where it was dry, foods made of flour such as noodles and dumplings were eaten because they help moisten the skin and internal organs. In Sichuan Province, where it was rainy, more chillies were eaten to help dispel dampness. The newspaper ran TCM cures for everything from smelly feet, to acne, to leukaemia and heart disease. It also detailed many of the weird and wonderful TCM recipes and explained the TCM timeframe for daily living. It turned out TCM is quite obsessed with defecating. In a newspaper where the niceties of language were often overlooked in translation, it led to a series of what I considered quite squirm-inducing stories on the subject of bowel movements. Maintaining a 24-hour health schedule is important in Traditional Chinese Medicine which breaks the day into twelve, two-hour units. It was all about moving qi in your body. For the record, for optimum health and energy flow, TCM dictates you should move your bowels between 5 a.m. and 7 a.m. daily. And you should never hold your breath while doing so.

TCM was experiencing something of a revival in Shanghai. District level hospitals across the city had begun including treatment and advice based on TCM as part of their service, including therapies such as herbal soup, exercise, music therapy, acupuncture and massage. But there were only 270 000 TCM doctors in China, and only 30 000 of the doctors practised TCM exclusively. As a result, there was a push to ensure more doctors were trained in the field as well as to incorporate it into the Chinese medical mainstream.

It so happened there was a TCM hospital near where we lived in Jing'an. With a note written by a colleague, on which she promised she had written in Chinese 'this man has a sore neck', Smarty headed off for his first TCM experience. After entering Yue Yang Hospital on Qinghai Lu, he delivered his note to a nurse. She asked him to pay 15 yuan (A$2.40) and led him to what he thought was the sore neck and back room. The room was in an old, high-ceilinged building and was about 8 metres wide by 20 metres long, packed with eight beds, four doctors, 22 patients, two children and a microwave in the middle of the room that kept going bing to alert the nurses their noodles were ready. Smarty could see no queuing system in operation, so followed the locals' lead and sat on one of the numerous little stools around the room as soon as the opportunity arose. Everyone appeared keen to have a chat. They might have been walking around in their underpants in readiness for treatment, but none were seemingly missing out on the opportunity to pass comment on any given topic. Smarty sensed he may be the butt of quite a few comments and outbursts of laughter, but still he stuck to his stool and waited for a doctor to notice him.

He assessed the four doctors working the room. He told me he nicknamed them Elvis, the Gangster, the Scientist and the Kid. Elvis spied Smarty and claimed him as his patient. Elvis had smooth skin, perfect hair, a belly like a marshmallow and hands and forearms Superman would be proud of. In halting English he revealed to Smarty that he worked 15 hours a day, six days a week. When Smarty told him he was Australian, Elvis confided that he really liked Australian biscuits (or at least that's what Smarty thought he said).

The Scientist was a woman who appeared in her mid-40s and looked like she was born to wear a long white coat. She wore her hair back in a Chinese clip and had black rimmed glasses. She looked very intense. The Kid was smiley and spent his time bounding merrily from patient to patient. Smarty's favourite, though, was the Gangster. He was craggy and weather-beaten and looked like a Mafia henchman, only he was Chinese. His favourite massage trick was to get a sausage-like apparatus that looked like a door snake and whack people with it. It was all part of his treatment. Some patients allowed themselves a little squeal, but it elicited no sympathy whatsoever. The Gangster appeared to live by his own rules. Smarty said he occasionally stopped work and, in the middle of the 'surgery', pulled out a cigarette and lit it up. He was a multi-skilled doctor it would seem, able to draw heavily on his cigarette, blow smoke around the room, sip a cup of tea, and give someone a bit of a one-handed neck rub all at the same time. But that was not all. Smarty said that an electrician, busy at work on an air conditioning unit, decided to wander across the room to have a chat with the multi-skilling Gangster. The conversation degenerated into a Chinese shout-fest. The electrician began waving dirty wiring around with his filthy hands, the Gangster fired back while never missing a beat on the person he was treating. The patient he was working on then bought into the argument herself. Meanwhile, other patients kept wandering around, adding their own comments and jumping on any treatment stools that became available as the microwave kept binging, bringing nurses scurrying in to fetch their hot snacks. Amid the pandemonium, the electrician, seemingly rebuked on the finer points of electrical wiring by the Gangster and his patient, marched back to the air conditioner in the corner, just missing stepping into the puddle of wee one of the nappy-less children had left as a calling card in the middle of the floor.

Smarty said his session with Elvis really made a difference to his sore neck. He headed back for two follow-up sessions, I think largely because he enjoyed sitting and watching the drama around him so much. He took a packet of Australia's most popular plain sweet biscuit, Arnott's Scotch Fingers, as a thank-you gift. Elvis accepted them with a quizzical look. Perhaps he didn't say biscuits after all.

CHAPTER 14

DON'T TELL ME NOT TO PANIC

In China, there were times when I just wanted the facts. Selfishly, it was the times when my family's own health or lives were affected that I had no time for the way the Chinese media works. In March, an outbreak of the normally routine children's illness, hand, foot and mouth disease (HFMD), began killing children.

The cause was found to be a lethal intestinal virus called enterovirus 71 (EV71). EV71 can cause hand, foot and mouth disease. It usually starts with a slight fever followed by blisters and ulcers in the mouth and rashes on the hands and feet. It also can cause high fever, meningitis, inflammation of the brain called encephalitis, fluid on the lungs called pulmonary oedema, and paralysis. There is no vaccine.

The *Shanghai Daily* covered the story. The epidemic was first reported on March 20 in Fuyang City in Anhui Province in east China. Outbreaks were subsequently reported elsewhere in China. By May 6, 26 children had died. Just about all were below six years of age. There were 1314 children in hospitals with the virus. In Anhui, 5840 children were reported to be infected with HFMD. Anhui had suffered 22 of the deaths. The southern province of Guangdong was dealing with 1692 reported cases. Three boys in the province had died so far in the outbreak. Zhejiang Province in east China had recorded 1198 children with the disease since January. A five-year-old boy in the province died on April 6. In southwestern Chongqing Municipality, 42 cases had been detected in just one week. Beijing had recorded 1482 cases, and the capital's neighbouring Hebei Province had reported 206 infections. There were also cases being monitored in the provinces of Jiangsu, Hunan, Hubei, Shaanxi, Jiangxi and Henan.

The May 6 report said there were no cases of the fatal HFMD yet in Shanghai. Mothers I was in contact with were getting extremely worried. A number had *ayi* who were Anhui native and who had returned home for Golden Week holidays. The mothers were concerned their *ayi* may be carrying the disease – adults do not necessarily show symptoms, but can be carriers – and the mothers did not know whether to have their *ayi* tested or stand them down during the epidemic. There was general concern at the number of people our children would come into contact with, as many migrant workers in Shanghai hailed from Anhui. Chinese mothers told me many children were being kept home from local kindergartens, which was where most of the victims contracted the disease. Numbers even dropped at the playgroup I attended with the kids, which had mostly Australian members.

The paper continued to run stories on the progress of the epidemic. Xinhua copy predictably contained praise for the Chinese government's handling of the outbreak. On May 6, the same day it was reported 26 children had died, Xinhua filed: 'World Health Organization representative in China, Hans Troedsson, has expressed appreciation for China's quick response to the outbreak of hand-foot-mouth disease (HFMD) and pledged the world body's willingness to support China in its efforts to combat the illness.'

At work on May 8, I received a story to edit that the potentially fatal EV71 had arrived in Shanghai. The copy I was given had been sourced to the transcript of an online interview with unnamed local health officials. There were no details of when the disease was found in Shanghai, where, how it had got there, what condition the patient was in, or any details about the patient. Instead the anonymous officials told the public there was no need to panic. The story also said HFMD was a common disease and prevention and treatment could control any outbreak in the city.

I immediately called the reporter and told her she needed more details. I said the story angle telling people not to worry when they had no real information other than that a child-killing disease had arrived in the city was nonsense. She said there were no more details on the online transcript, so there was nothing she could add. I asked to her to make some phone calls to health authorities, hospitals or perhaps kindergartens to get some real information. She said she would call me back. And didn't. A chief overheard my conversation and argued that there was no proof that EV71 was a fatal form of HFMD or that it was actually responsible for all the child deaths. He said that was why nobody should be overly concerned. I did not get involved in the argument. I took my concerns to the editor. The editor was concerned that my complaints about the copy meant we would have no story for the page. The story was taken out of my hands.

I read the approved copy in the paper the next day:

'The Shanghai Center for Disease Control and Prevention has detected Enterovirus 71, an intestinal virus causing a nationwide outbreak of hand-foot-mouth disease that has killed 28 children, in the city, local health officials said in an online interview.

'It is the first time that Shanghai officials said they have found EV71 cases in the city.

'HFMD is a common virus and medical authorities told the public not to panic because proper prevention and early treatment can control the spread of the disease. The virus usually only infects young children.

'"As of Monday, the city had reported 1988 HFMD cases without a fatality or critically ill patient. There were some 10 700 HFMD cases last year and none suffered severe symptoms," said Xu Jianguang, director of the Shanghai Health Bureau.'

I considered trying to find out more information myself. I figured parents like me across Shanghai would want to know how sick the victim was and how and where they had caught the disease. I wanted to know who they had come into contact with and how the disease could be spreading. I wanted to know what the parents did to prevent their child getting HFMD, what they did wrong, and what we could all learn from their experience. It was not good enough that our kids could be in danger of contracting a potentially fatal disease just by going to kindergarten and we wouldn't be comforted by anonymous government officials telling us not to worry. Before I picked up the phone and caused all sorts of trouble for myself, I realised the folly of trying to make my own enquiries and perhaps providing real information to *Shanghai Daily* readers. The newspaper was, of course, running all the information it had been approved to run.

By May 10, the national death toll from the outbreak was 34 and the number of cases nationwide had risen to more than 27 600. A fourteen-month-old boy and an eighteen-month-old girl, both in Anhui, were the latest victims. Experts confirmed EV71 killed the two babies. The virus had also been confirmed as the cause of death for most of the other 32 fatalities. We still had no details about the Shanghai sufferer. Friends of mine told me at least one Chinese kindergarten a few blocks from where I lived had closed down due to HFMD. I kept sending Milly to kindy, thinking I couldn't keep her trapped inside the apartment all day and to take her out anywhere else in public would likely put her more at risk than in the kindergarten environment. Her kindergarten, along with all local and private kindergartens in Shanghai, had started checking children for signs of the illness as they arrived for the day. Each child's hands were slathered in antiseptic gel as they arrived and their hands, feet and mouths checked for blisters or a rash. The newspaper said medical experts were predicting a further rise in infections as the disease's peak season was traditionally in June and July. The experts said they were working on a vaccine.

Among my network of mothers there was simmering anger and panic over the epidemic. We were well aware we were guests in another country and therefore must accept the way that country handles information dissemination and emergencies such as outbreaks of killer diseases. I was acutely conscious of the dearth of information being presented in the English language media. Our children were at risk. There was no authority to complain to. The best we could do was vent our frustrations to each other. At work, I didn't get to edit any more of the stories on HFMD.

The *Shanghai Daily* finally reported the death of a child from HFMD in the city: 'Shanghai Health Bureau reported a fatal case of hand, foot and mouth disease yesterday. The dead boy is the first person to have died of HFMD in the city, where the epidemic has been controlled.' The victim was two years old and identified only as Yu. He was from Shangshui County in Henan Province and had been living in Shanghai's Songjiang District. He died at the Shanghai Public Health Centre, hours after arriving at hospital. He was confirmed as having HFMD with viral encephalitis.

The boy's death was not front page news. It was not followed up. Another far greater emergency struck China. On May 12, an earthquake registering 8 on the Richter scale struck Sichuan Province. The lives of more than 80 000 people were lost in the disaster.

CHAPTER 15

MAY 12, 2008

It started with a white-knuckle taxi ride to get Milly to kindy, which meant it was a typical Monday morning. After depositing Milly at Mother Goose, I'd taken Nelson to an art class in a lovely old apartment down an alley in the violin-making section of leafy Fuxing Lu in the French Concession. It's where he'd get to paint, spread glue and glitter and scrunch paper and get himself and the floor covered in colour. And I didn't have to clean up. After the class I'd returned with Nelson to collect Milly, taken both kids home in another taxi, given them lunch and popped them into bed for a nap. While I was trotting around with the children, Smarty was at work having a reasonably busy day. He decided rather than going to lunch with colleagues at a local restaurant, he'd just duck across Weihei Lu to grab a bowl of wantons.

Back in the building, he suddenly felt woozy, slightly nauseous and dizzy. He feared his wanton lunch was having a swift and negative effect. Others around him complained of the same sensation. Suddenly, one of the *Shanghai Daily* deputy editors rounded the corner from the news section, shouting, 'The building is moving, we have to get out!' One of Smarty's colleagues, a Scot named Doug, said he was not waiting around to be a hero. He headed for the stairs. Smarty followed. Amid much shrieking and nervous chatter, the paper's editorial staff funnelled from the 38th floor down the narrow staircase usually used as an unofficial smoking room. Staff from the other newspaper headquarters in the building were also using the same staircase and trying to reach the safety of street level before the building started to crumble. None of the offices seemed to have any sort of evacuation plan.

At street level, Smarty ran into thousands of other workers who had poured onto the footpaths from buildings all around the district. Together they waited, watching their office towers with a mixture of fear and excitement over what would happen. All felt the sway. It was an earthquake, yet nobody knew any more details. It occurred to Smarty, and others, that standing in the street as buildings collapsed might not be the safest place to be. Briefly, he considered going back inside. After about an hour, without any engineer or building expert's assessment, *Shanghai Daily* management told staff the building was safe and they needed to return to work. Before he followed everyone back inside, Smarty called me to check if the kids and I were okay. I told him we'd been asleep. I had no idea what had gone on. I was immediately anxious about the safety of the kids. I didn't know whether to stay in the apartment. I'd seen how quickly buildings go up in Shanghai and suspected they hadn't all been built to quake-proof standards. But I couldn't imagine where would be safer. We chatted nervously about our brush with an earthquake, my ability to sleep through anything and Smarty's confusion between the earth shaking and a batch of dodgy wantons. The jokes made me feel a whole lot calmer and Smarty recounted the excitement the tremor caused downtown. I was actually a bit disappointed I missed it. Then I switched on the news.

At 2.28 p.m. a magnitude 8.0 earthquake hit Wenchuan County in China's south-western Sichuan Province. Aftershocks had been felt across much of the country, including Shanghai and as far away as Vietnam. The earthquake had caused devastation. There was chaos and confusion. Slowly, the full extent of the drama, the loss of human life, the fear and the destruction unfolded. It was a catastrophe. It was a tragedy so massive it was difficult for foreigners or locals to comprehend, but May 12 would be scarred into the nation's psyche. It was expected the quake would be even more devastating than the 7.8-magnitude quake in 1976 in Tangshan city, northern Hebei Province, which claimed more than 240 000 lives. And the extent of the damage in Sichuan was only just coming to light.

By Tuesday, the death toll stood at 12 000. Another 18 000 were missing. More than 15 million people lived in the quake zone. Almost 4 million lived in the capital city of Sichuan Province, Chengdu. Reports said almost 2000 of the dead were students and teachers killed when their school buildings collapsed.

Previously all I had really known of Sichuan Province was its fiery cuisine and famous panda sanctuary. Now it was a disaster zone, full of flattened towns and cities and precarious mountains and valleys that had swallowed buildings, roads and schools. Men, women and children who were going about their daily lives had perished in extraordinary numbers. We were living more than 1600 kilometres away, but I had never been so close to such a large-scale disaster, such immense suffering.

As is so often the case with tragedy on a grand scale, it is rarely the big numbers that help us understand the damage and the pain. It is only when we hear individual stories that we can even begin to get a sense of the devastation. China's media – at least the English-language media, and in particular the *Shanghai Daily* – was generally very poor at telling stories about people. Normally, it was all about government and numbers. But individual stories of loss and distress, of people suffering, trying to cope, their acts of heroism and grief, soon came pouring out of Sichuan.

Wu Jiafang said he wanted to preserve the dignity of his dead wife. The photograph of Wu riding his motorbike with his wife's body bound to his back after retrieving her from the crumpled remains of the building where she died to take her home to be buried was a portrait of misery. The image of Wu and others from the quake zone were put on display in the lobby of our media office tower. They showed some people coping, some grieving and some looking totally lost. They were horribly captivating. It was pictures like these that were even more overwhelming than the grotesque images of bodies, including dead babies, being pulled from the rubble that some papers, including the *China Daily*, published on their front page. In the lobby there were pictures of survivors, of exhausted rescuers, of faces filled with horror and despair, of some filled with relief and gratitude. There were also haunting pictures of rows of little school bags beside ruins where school buildings once stood. Nearly 14 000 schools in Sichuan Province collapsed or were damaged in the quake. The little school bags would never be claimed.

I was drawn daily to a picture of one woman. She had a face dirty and grimy from the ruins, but she had a smile. Her face wasn't bursting with joy, but it showed hope. She was cradling a baby and breastfeeding the infant. She was wearing a police officer's uniform. The woman was Jiang Xiaojuan. Jiang started breast-feeding nine infant quake survivors to keep them alive. She left her own six-month-old son with his grandparents who could only feed him powdered milk as she tended to the nine quake babies. Weeks after the quake, Jiang Xiaojuan had to be treated for the psychological damage inflicted by the earthquake disaster. She said she could not escape feelings of guilt about her own son and was trying to block out the memories of the horrific experience. There is little doubt she saved nine babies.

The story of another mother in the city of Dujiangyan, south-east of the quake's epicentre, triggered tears across the nation. Found by rescuers in a strange kneeling position with her upper body hunched forward supported by her outstretched arms, the woman was covered in bricks and debris. When discovered, she was already dead. The rescuers moved on. But something drew the team leader back. He moved closer and reached through the wreckage to check underneath her body. Underneath the arch of her torso, in a tiny pocket of safe space, he found her baby. Wrapped in a red quilt dotted with yellow flowers, the three-month-old baby lay sleeping, completely uninjured. When the baby was pulled clear, it was handed to a doctor to be examined. The doctor unfolded the baby's quilt, and a mobile phone dropped out. On the screen there was a text message: 'My dear baby, if you survive, remember I love you.' The doctor, who had seen so many terrible images since the earthquake struck, burst into tears. The phone was passed around the rescue team. And the tears flowed. On reading the story, so did mine. I found it was the stories of children and the extent to which their mothers, fathers and grandparents sacrificed to ensure a child's survival that were the stories that affected me most. The numbers of the dead were too overwhelming to have an impact any more. But one mum's efforts to save her baby hit home and I couldn't help but tear up. It was no longer like the earthquake was only affecting the Chinese. I'd lost that distance between 'us' and 'them'. I pulled the kids into bed with me when I got home from work that night. China, and our life, didn't feel quite so safe any more.

In the face of such overwhelming loss, we felt almost incapable of offering help. We donated money through the newspaper and at collection points throughout the city. The donations were reportedly spent providing survivors with tents, blankets, food and medical supplies. Official figures showed Chinese and foreign donors contributed cash and goods worth about 75.2 billion yuan (A\$12.25 billion) for relief and rehabilitation in the six months following the earthquake. But so much of what survivors of a tragedy like this really need does not come in cash or care packages. They need their lives to be safe again.

The official toll, announced by Premier Wen Jiabao, stood at more than 80 000 people. Wen said rescuers pulled 84 000 survivors from shattered buildings. He said Chinese authorities relocated 15 million people and treated at least 96 000 injured victims at hospitals. The earthquake also all but wiped out an entire Chinese sub-culture. One in 10 Qiang, a minority nationality of 300 000 people in Sichuan, died in the quake. The Qiang people have a history traced to the Shang Dynasty (1600–1046 BC). Known as the 'people in the white clouds' because they usually live in ornately decorated stone houses in the upper reaches of the mountains, the Qiang led a simple existence herding sheep and growing crops such as corn and cherries. Their culture had been carried through the generations by individuals known as *xu* or *shibi*. Among the dead were more than 40 official cultural carriers.

Some of the overall death toll were victims of aftershocks, floods and landslides. Within weeks of the earthquake, some areas of the quake zone were hit with the heaviest rainfalls they had experienced for 100 years. Thousands of people, many in make-shift shelters, were evacuated from their temporary homes due to the rains. A further 200 000 people were relocated and more than 1 million others warned to make evacuation plans when authorities decided to drain a lake formed by the earthquake that was threatening to burst its banks. The lake, called Tangjiashan, occurred when a hillside plunged into a river valley during the quake. I couldn't imagine what other catastrophe could beset these people.

Yet somehow, China started to recover. The country grieved but moved on. We became numb to the numbers that were so shocking when the earthquake occurred. Students returned to studying and exams. Buildings sprang up again from the rubble. Farmers replanted in the altered landscape. And there was an Olympic Games to show the world.

I found it almost shocking the way the country actually managed to confine the human tragedy to the past and focused instead on the financial toll, judging the international response and detailing the government's own recovery efforts. A few characters from the earthquake, however, still managed to become a national obsession. A teacher named Fan Meizhong became nationally reviled for his cowardice. Fan became known as 'Run Run Fan' and had his teaching licence revoked after he admitted abandoning his students in the quake aftermath. In an interview just days after the May 12 quake, Fan said: 'I ran as fast as I could, almost on all fours, to the football field. I found myself the first person there. I didn't see any of my students.' When his students finally found their way to the field and asked Fan why he didn't help them, he reportedly said: ' I'm not the sort of person who is ready to sacrifice his life. I care only about my own life.' He told his students: 'Although I strive for freedom and fairness, I will not sacrifice myself to help others. At this critical time of life and death, I can only think about sacrificing myself for my daughter. I will not consider saving anyone else, not even my mother. I am not strong enough to carry an adult out of danger.' Fan was sacked. While he has been unable to teach again in China, the earthquake made him something of a Chinese celebrity.

As it did a pig. A miracle pig. The pig was found on June 17 after surviving 36 days under rubble from the earthquake living on charcoal and rainwater. It was bought by a local museum that spent more than 6000 yuan (A$978) purchasing the pig, transporting it and building it a new sty. Chinese media reported that museum officials called the pig 'a witness of the earthquake' and 'a miracle of life' and said that they would keep it as a 'cultural relic' until it died naturally. They named the pig, 'Zhu Jianqiang' or 'Mr Strong Willed'.

But it was a ten-year-old boy who became the face of China's earthquake heroes. Lin Hao was attending Yuzixi Primary School in quake-epicentre-Wenchuan County when the earthquake struck. Lin not only survived the earthquake, but after getting out of his classroom charged back into the wreckage to pull two classmates to safety. During the rescue, he was hit by falling debris and suffered injuries to his arms and head. While his classmates (ten survivors out of 32 students) were waiting for help, he encouraged them to sing songs to keep their spirits up. When he was asked why he risked his life, he said: 'I was the hall monitor, it was my job to look after my classmates.'

Lin was selected to walk with China's flag bearer Yao Ming around the National Stadium at the Opening Ceremony of the Beijing Olympics on August 8. Another child who survived the earthquake opened the Paralympics Opening Ceremony. She too reminded us that above all, the Sichuan earthquake was a tragedy about people, not productivity or the stock market. Wearing a single red ballet shoe, eleven-year-old Li Yue performed a wheelchair ballet to open the Games. It was just months after her leg was amputated without the help of pain killers so she could be pulled from her collapsed school building. Li was the only survivor of her class after her school building crumbled during the quake. Rescuers had almost given up hope of finding any more survivors after 40 hours of searching, but were alerted to Li when she used her electronic watch to blip light signals up through the pile of collapsed concrete. When rescuers reached Li, they told her she would either have to lose her leg or her life. She drank almost a bottle of vinegar before the amputation operation, her only defence against the pain of survival. When she danced at the Paralympic Opening Ceremony, it was with the uninhibited joy of a little girl.

Children can adapt. Parents who have lost a child do what they can. There was one part of the post-earthquake recovery that reminded me that we were nowhere but China. Following the quake, Sichuan Province passed a regulation to allow families who lost their children in the May 12 earthquake to have more children. The rule stated a family who lost an only child, or in which the child was disabled, or a family with two children who were both disabled in the disaster, could have a baby. A one-child family in which either the husband or wife was disabled, could also have a baby. It was a massive alteration to the strict one-child policy. It was an immensely popular decision. It was also something that would never cross my mind were I not living in China. I felt for the parents but, as a mother, couldn't imagine feeling a need to replace a child who died. About 18 000 families lost children in the quake. Two to three days after the earthquake, some parents went to family planning authorities to check if there were any new birth policies so they could have a new baby.

On February 17, 2009, nine months after the death of their only daughter, Yang Xia and Xian Ziwen became the first bereaved parents from the quake zone to have a second child. Their daughter, 19-year-old Xian Juan, died in the May 12 earthquake. Their new baby girl was seen across China as another symbol of the province's emergence from the ruins of the disaster. It made me feel increasingly detached from the tragedy. I felt removed from the wreckage of the earthquake by virtue of being so far away in Shanghai, a foreigner, and a non-Chinese speaker, but also the reaction of the Chinese. It seemed the response to the earthquake by so many Chinese had been to show the world their efficiency at managing a disaster and their ability to move forward. Of course, my information was coming via the English-language media and through contact with local people in Shanghai, among whom few had relatives or friends in the quake zone. They too seemed disconnected from the ongoing suffering of so many people so far away and rushed to get on with their own busy lives. Of course nothing could be done for the 80 000 people in Sichuan who died. But scars couldn't heal that quickly for the survivors.

It seemed to me an offence to these survivors when Chinese tourism authorities began promoting some of the earthquake ruins as a tourist site. Within about two years of the disaster, Beichuan County in Sichuan Province planned to set up tourist facilities at the quake zone including a lookout point at Sandaoguai Mountain. Officials said the lookout would give tourists a good overall view of the ruins. Tourists could then visit the site of Beichuan Middle School where more than 1200 students and teachers died. On the list of attractions was also expected to be a museum of a Qiang Ethnic Minority Village to remember a lost culture.

CHAPTER 16

ONLINE ARMY

The May 12 earthquake cut all telephone communication to Sichuan Province. As the news of the quake spread, thousands of Sichuan natives tried desperately to call home in search of family and friends. One soldier, who was being trucked to the epicentre of Wenchuan, lost contact with his seven-months' pregnant wife in Jiangyou County, another of the badly hit areas in Sichuan Province. The soldier posted a letter on Chinese Internet sites on May 13 asking for help to find his wife, Wang Zhuo. On Sina.com, the country's largest online portal, the online community ran a campaign to help find the *Junsao* (a term of respect for a soldier's wife). Thousands responded. Many called the Jiangyou Public Security Bureau which sent 10 police officers to search for the 25-year-old woman. But it was Internet users in Jiangyou who had also seen the call for help who got out of their homes and found her two days later. She was sheltering in a cement pipe and was fast running out of drinking water. She was taken to the local police bureau where she posted her thanks to her rescuers online and let her husband know she was alive.

In China, members of the Internet community are known as netizens. I was told by work colleagues that China's Internet population was 298 million and the country had about 50 million bloggers. On the newspaper I had handled many stories quoting netizens and initially wondered why often anonymous Internet bloggers were having their comments taken so seriously as to warrant being quoted in the news pages of a metropolitan daily. I began to realise that the comments were not just by the odd Internet user, but a whole tide of netizens. This army of faceless newsbreaking bloggers and Internet users were making real contributions to the information available to everyday Chinese citizens and it just couldn't be ignored. In the face of heavily controlled media, netizens were becoming China's taskforce for transparency of government, providing real opinions and rallying action. I know it sounds terrible, but it was a disaster of the magnitude of the Sichuan earthquake that allowed the netizen phenomenon to really shine. From the perspective of a media observer in China, I found it exciting.

As the earthquake struck Sichuan, not only did China's netizens unite to find missing people such as the soldier's wife, they dominated mainstream reporting of the tragedy. Netizens became pivotal in getting genuine information and pictures of the quake zone out nationally and internationally, well before conventional media. The first stories and pictures of the disaster appeared on Internet websites about 20 minutes after the first rumblings of the massive quake. Within four hours of the earthquake, there were over 30 million searches on the Wenchuan earthquake in China's main search engines. The vice-president of Xinhua News Agency and president of its online arm Xinhuanet, Zhou Xisheng, said he had never experienced anything like it. Relief workers, volunteers and survivors in the quake zone put their words and pictures from mobile phones and cameras straight on to the Internet, psychologists and rescue experts who could not make their way to the disaster area offered expertise online, netizens established lists of the missing and the found for families and friends cut off from their loved ones, government officials even took to the online chat rooms to answer questions by netizens about the earthquake and the rescue and relief effort. Some Internet sites established online donation registers, several web media jointly built the Wenchuan Earthquake Online Memorial Hall and launched the online public memorial for the quake victims. Through the Internet, netizens sent flowers, wrote messages and expressed their condolences for the dead and comforted those still alive.

Netizens also directed rescue helicopters and trucks carrying aid to safe places to land and navigated them past roads and bridges cut off or destroyed in the earthquake. Teams of netizens constantly ran information on traffic around Chengdu as relief poured into the Sichuan capital. Netizens also posted lists of schools and the classrooms that collapsed in the quake. Almost 4800 students perished in the quake when their schools and classrooms crumbled.

A further 16 000 were injured, according to the Education Ministry. The shocking numbers, overwhelming parental grief and a campaign by netizens outraged at the number of children killed while they were at school led to an investigation into the construction standards of schools in China and a new code of school building standards.

Within one week of the quake, more than 250 000 entries from the disaster zone were posted to the top three blog sites in China, attracting 2 billion page views. Thousands of home videos were posted on China's video sharing websites such as Tudou.com and 6 million Chinese added a rainbow to their MSN signatures to show their support and solidarity with the Sichuan victims. Others offered support for the earthquake orphans. More than 300 netizens across the country submitted adoption applications to civil affairs authorities in Sichuan Province to take in one of the more than 200 children who lost their entire families in the quake. Other netizens listed their incomes, residences, professions and contact details so they could be called upon to help the children.

The effect on China's traditional media was astounding. Many media commentators said official print and television news reporting of the quake was deeper and broader than any event in Chinese history. It had to be. Official media was no longer in control of the story. At the *Shanghai Daily* we saw the paper forced to report the human stories, many often translated straight from the netizen reportage. As a newspaper reader accustomed to detail rather than broadbrush statistics and rawness of emotion rather than rhetoric, I found the netizen influence vital in making the paper's coverage of the earthquake worth bothering with. The story, by Chinese standards, was out of control. Netizens kept pushing traditional boundaries on the stories coming out of Sichuan and proved to be the truest source of information. Far more than anything the government could have orchestrated, netizens made the rest of China and the world care about Sichuan. And through the sheer volume of netizen contributions and the accessibility of the information, the Chinese government knew it had lost its normally tight control and that people were watching as it responded to the emergency and suffering of its people.

Netizens monitored all aspects of the government response. When tents sent to quake victims started to appear in areas where temporary shelters were not needed, netizens blew the whistle. The government was forced to act on officials embezzling relief funds and supplies. The Internet also shaped the efforts of corporate donors. Sina.com ranked corporate donations, attracting a flood of comments to online bulletin boards about companies who did and did not make the lists. Foreign companies in particular came under heavy fire in the rankings and online opinion. Many netizens considered multinationals cashing in on the eager and populous market offered by China for their products, needed to show a greater corporate social responsibility in China's time of crisis. They even called for a ban on some products whose parent company they thought had not offered the quake victims enough financial help. Their postings had an impact. Many companies doubled or even tripled their donations of cash and goods after faring poorly in the online ranking system.

Netizens fed on snippets from the disaster zone, acted as advocates for victim's rights and analysed the government's and the world's response with intelligence and forthright opinion, as well as getting stuck in to the occasional bit of loopiness. When Sharon Stone opened her mouth to utter her bizarre and offensive comment that the Sichuan earthquake was karma for China's human rights record in Tibet, netizens let loose. For a brief moment, the gaffe-prone actress sapped everyone's attention. It was like the real stories of the earthquake ceased to exist for a time as everybody – netizens and the mainstream media – indulged in one of their favourite topics: bashing the West for criticising China. Netizens led the condemnation of the actress. 'I'm not happy about the way the Chinese are treating the Tibetans because I don't think anyone should be unkind to anyone else,' Stone said in a red carpet interview. 'And then this earthquake and all this stuff happened, and then I thought, is this karma? When you're not nice that the bad things happen to you?' The comments were dim-witted and beyond insulting to the thousands of quake victims and their families. But they really could have just been taken as the daft ramblings of a former movie star. But in China, nothing that can be taken as an insult to the government or its people is allowed to go through to the keeper. China reacted as though Sharon Stone was vocalising the sentiments of the US and the West. Furious netizens stormed the online bulletin boards, condemning Stone's comments and calling for her movies to be banned from all Chinese cinemas. I'm sure the government couldn't have been happier. If there's one sure way to boost Chinese nationalism and encourage the Chinese people to turn to their government for assurance, it is to tell the Chinese people they are being picked on by the ignorant West. Ultimately, the Shanghai International Film Festival permanently banned Stone and her films and Christian Dior dropped her from its Chinese advertising campaign. Stone apologised. And unsure what other recourse could be taken against the actress, China's netizens and the rest of the country turned their attention back to the real victims in Sichuan.

The earthquake was the critical point at which netizens cemented their role as news leaders and opinion shapers in China. It was the moment netizens took on and performed the function that, in the West, we consider part of the job of journalists and a free press. It emboldened many of China's citizens who needed nothing more than a computer to share information, to offer aid, to condemn or applaud. In the wake of the earthquake, netizens became empowered. They uncovered lies and corruption and brought people information they would otherwise not have access to. It was the kind of change I'd been hoping to see in China's press. I had thought that I might see the opening up of 'new China' reflected in a freer and more questioning mainstream media during my time in Shanghai. I quickly found that was not to be the case on the *Shanghai Daily*. Within a week on the job I had resigned myself to the media operating as the propaganda tool of government. So I was very excited to see the emergence of netizens and the information that they were channelling out through the Internet crossover onto the mainstream news pages.

Of course the Internet in China is nowhere close to a free-for-all and the country's noose of censorship still hangs over netizens. Netizens often have to resort to code words to pass through what is dubbed the Great Firewall of China, which operates to detect and deter anyone publishing, downloading or even reading articles and reports that possibly undermine or challenge the government or its power. Special hardware and programs have been put in place to spot offending material and identify the user as well as an army of censors who trawl through China's most popular online forums and blogs identifying and erasing banned words and topics. I can't come close to understanding the detail of how such highly technical online censorship works, but figure the policing of the Internet is akin to a massive version of the way home filters stop kids accessing what are deemed inappropriate websites. All this filtering and censoring made using the Internet in China highly frustrating. Websites that were accessible one day were blocked the next. My email account was occasionally impossible to access. And I didn't ever dare conduct searches on China's most sensitive topics such as Tibet, Tiananmen and Taiwan for fear the computer itself would explode. Some argue that the Internet is still so tightly controlled in China that the rise of the netizens phenomenon does little to bring the country any closer to democracy. They say the Communist Party actually gives netizens a bit of leash so bloggers can blow off steam online, rather than actually forging or organising any real change. I understand the argument, but remain hopeful I was witness to a shift towards a greater flow of information. I'm quite sure I was, even if in real terms it was only a small development.

Netizens like 'Ghost 2009' showed just how effectively the Internet in China could be used by this army of 'citizen journalists'. In the real world 'Ghost 2009' is a mild mannered IT worker, according to the China Youth Daily that tracked him down. But in the cyber world he is an anti-corruption superhero. 'Ghost 2009' posted on the Internet a series of photographs and documents that showed Chinese officials had been abusing public funds on trips to

Las Vegas and Niagara Falls. He found the swag of documents on a subway in Shanghai. As soon as he posted the evidence, netizens swamped message boards demanding action. The story gathered pace. It made the leap to the mainstream media. The Party had no option but to act against the freeloading officials. As a result, two top officials were sacked while the other nine travellers were ordered to write self-criticism essays and repay the bills.

The Internet was also the medium which was used to bring an abusive, bullying official to justice. A Communist Party official in Shenzhen accused of abusing an eleven-year-old girl in a restaurant bathroom was forced to resign after netizens posted security camera footage online that showed him waving off the girl's distraught family when they confronted him moments after the incident. It also showed him taunting them with his Party rank to get them to drop their complaint. Again, the story began on the Internet. It was netizens who pursued the allegations, sought out the evidence and presented it for the public to see. The mainstream media reported the result.

My favourite story of netizens doing the investigative work of the media, though, had to be the famous case of the rare South China tiger sighting in China's north-west Shaanxi Province. It was netizens who first expressed scepticism over the South China tiger sighting by a farmer named Zhou Zhenglong. Farmer Zhou claimed he had seen and had photographs to prove the existence of a South China tiger believed to be extinct in the wild. He released his photograph and local forestry officials backed up the authenticity of the image. But netizens weren't convinced. Usually in China when officials declare something to be a fact, that is the end of the argument. But netizens remained dogged in their efforts to expose Zhou's ruse. They found an old Lunar New Year poster showing a tiger that looked the same as the one in Zhou's photo and claimed the 'proof' of the tiger in the wild was just digital trickery. Images of Zhou's tiger and the poster were displayed online. The story took off. Police were forced to act on the claims the photos were fake. When they searched Zhou's house they found not only an old tiger poster but a wooden model of a tiger paw Zhou allegedly used to make footprints in the snow.

Zhou was arrested and sentenced to two-and-a-half years in prison with a three-year reprieve. The scandal also brought down thirteen government staff in Shaanxi who were either sacked or reprimanded for their involvement in the scam. China's netizens had claimed another victory in the pursuit of truth.

CHAPTER 17

CHINA'S OLYMPICS

By summer, Shanghai was changing. The Olympics was going to be in Beijing in August, but the powerhouse city of Shanghai certainly didn't want to miss out on the party. Millions of foreign tourists were expected to flood into Shanghai during the Beijing Olympic period. The Beijing Olympics had been described as 'China's coming-out party' and the capital had done everything it could to prepare. But Shanghai had been readying itself like a city waiting to be judged.

It was hard to avoid some of the on-the-ground changes that were being adopted to supposedly make the city more tourist-friendly. On Shanghai street corners, special traffic wardens started appearing in an effort to help the Chinese obey street crossing protocols that are second nature in many other nations. Crossing the street in China could be terrifying, especially for those unfamiliar with the country's chaos theory of pedestrian survival. There was only one rule: pedestrians rated much lower than anything on wheels. It took me months to develop the confidence and timing to march out into the traffic at the right moment, look the right way, and walk at the right speed. It took that long again to accept that making it to the opposite footpath did not mean I had successfully and safely crossed the road. Cyclists and motorbike riders also crossed the street with pedestrians before roaring off down the footpath, expecting anyone on foot to leap out of their way. They got very cranky when a woman with a pram blocked their way from the street to the sidewalk. I was absolutely in favour of the traffic wardens' insistence that bicycle and motorbike riders dismounted to cross the street. And that they didn't get to ride again on the footpath, scattering pedestrians as they went, at least until the wardens turned their backs.

My favourite of these traffic wardens was a tiny woman who was the crankiest looking person I had ever seen. She policed the corner of Shaanxi Bei Lu and Nanjing Lu in the evening peak hour which was about the time I headed to work each day. As soon as the green walk signal flashed, she exhorted the masses gathered on the corner to 'cross, cross'. She also had a whistle. I could hear her blowing it from blocks away. She blew it every few seconds as she gesticulated wildly. She was not at all impressed with the street-crossing prowess of the locals. I even saw her dragging people across the road in frustration when the walk signal turned green, despite traffic still streaming through the intersection.

Shanghai had also jumped upon a recommendation out of Beijing to touch up English translations ahead of the Games. The list of insensitive rules that caused us such amusement when we first arrived had been removed from cabs. The only signs in Shanghai taxis as the Olympics approached were in Chinese.

A special edict had also been issued regarding food and drink menus. The idea was to get rid of some of the more bizarre, frightening and hilarious translations on menus to make them sound more appetising to foreigners. 'Chicken without sexual life' and 'husband and wife's lung slice' were to be axed. These dishes were instead to be called 'steamed pullet' and 'beef and ox tripe in chilli sauce'. 'Red burned lion head' had also undergone a change to 'braised pork balls in soy sauce'. And 'bean curd made by a pock-marked woman' was to be less interestingly called *mapo tofu*.

Some of the Shanghai menus we saw had been changed as the Olympics neared. But it was satisfying that the local restaurants we most often frequented didn't seem to be affected by this desire to make their menus sound more appetising. We were still offered choices of 'sheep's penis', 'fried pigs ears' and 'spicy little yellow croakers'. I was actually quite pleased they hadn't been changed to sound more appetising, lest I order them.

Also out of Beijing was a call to clean up bad habits that are seen as offensive by visitors. Top of the list was spitting. Beijing officials in the lead-up to the Games proposed a 'no spitting day'. Officials said the move would complement a new monthly 'Queuing Day' and 'Seat Offering Day', designated by the Beijing municipal government. I couldn't believe the reaction among Shanghai locals and opinion writers, most of whom were affronted at the no-spitting request and defended their right to spit and spit often. The reaction was even more robust than that to suggestions smokers tone down their habit. Some claimed spitting was an ancient custom in China and had been cited in 5000-year-old Chinese proverbs. I found one of the proverbs as gross as the habit. 'We used to say that China is so large a country that one spit from every Chinese may drown all people in a small country, which shows we have a long tradition of spitting,' one defender of spitting said on Sina.com.

Cosmetic changes made to Beijing drew much attention in Shanghai. The air quality in the capital was a hot topic and the government promised athletes would get to breathe clean air during the Games. It meant taking half of the city's 3.3 million cars off the road, shutting down factories and cutting back on construction. About a month before the Games, Beijing implemented the plan that saw cars with odd-numbered licence plates banned one day, and even-numbered plates the next. The idea was floated that the measure be kept up permanently and expanded to other cities to battle the dense pollution in most Chinese urban areas. Despite the Games being held under the promised blue sky, the idea to allow city-dwellers to breathe a little more easily year-round didn't fly. No-one in go-ahead China, and certainly not in Shanghai, appeared to be keen on giving up any opportunity to drive their status-enhancing vehicles.

It was incredible to watch the certainty with which officials promised that China would deliver a successful Olympic Games. Apart from the blue sky guarantee and the promise that the spectacular Olympic venues, including the incomparable Bird's Nest, would be ready by the August 8 Opening Ceremony, officials assured the Chinese people and the world that the weather would be fine. Officials had been quoted in a national release as saying that if the weather turned out not to be fine, particularly for the Opening Ceremony, they had the technology to change it. Even more astonishingly, officials promised there would be no earthquakes at Games time.

The most farcical statement made by the Chinese in the lead-up to the Games, however, was that the Games would be open to foreign and local media. Offering expectations that the international media would be able to operate under similar freedoms to those they experienced at previous Olympics in Athens and Sydney, including unfettered access to the Internet, meant the issue was always going to be a fiasco. So too was the suggestion that local media would be able to report freely on the event. Nothing written concerning the Beijing Olympic Games had any chance of being free from rules and conditions imposed by the Propaganda Department. Not even 'foreign perspective' columns in the *Shanghai Daily*. Which was why I was banned.

I apparently flouted one of the Communist Party rulings. I had written a column in the lead-up to the Games discussing some of the pressures and expectations on athletes, especially Chinese gold medal hope in the 110 m hurdles and one of the faces of the Games, Liu Xiang. My column was spiked and I was banned from writing another word on the Olympics. I was told despite my Olympic experience and potential to offer some insight into the lead-up and running of the Games, I was to restrict any subsequent columns to amusing anecdotes about my kids and me in China. I wasn't extremely annoyed, more bemused, for this was China and arguing would change nothing. Thinking the column was really quite innocuous, I asked precisely what the order I breached had been. The *Shanghai Daily* opinion editor Wang Yong explained that the Propaganda Department had decided that, given the Olympic theme was 'One World, One Dream', it would not look good to foreigners if China went into the Olympics displaying an overt sense of nationalism and desire to perform well at the Games. The government, therefore, had issued a ruling that the Chinese public no longer expressly hoped their athletes would win, nor would they cheer fervently for Chinese athletes. Banners saying 'Go China' were banned and the central government issued an official four-part cheer, complete with approved actions, that spectators were to learn. The cheer 'Let's Go Olympics, Let's Go Beijing' was meant to reflect that the Chinese people would be pleased for all athletes and all nations who won gold medals. The department's pronouncement also meant that Chinese athletes, as a result of this generosity of sporting spirit, were no longer under any pressure from their countrymen to perform well at the Games. No-one was to suggest otherwise. Unfortunately, I didn't get the memo. I reasoned that an opinion piece was meant to contain an opinion and, in my opinion, the Chinese public might still be keen for their gold medal hopes to deliver the goods. I failed to be persuasive. My opinion was obviously the wrong one. My little column, banned for defying a Communist Party order, can be published here for the first time.

Cathy Freeman went from being a girl who just liked to run, to dragging the expectations of a nation and pride of a mistreated minority culture 400 m around an Olympic track.

Fani Halkia went from being a medal hope, to a woman tasked with returning dignity to the birthplace of the modern Olympics.

Liu Xiang will have nothing less than the desires of a fifth of humanity on his shoulders as he bounds 110 m in Beijing.

Sport so often is about so much more than just who comes first.

It wasn't hard to see the impact these 'extras' added to the burden Cathy Freeman carried in the Sydney 2000 Olympics.

As she crossed the finish line of the 400 m to claim gold, becoming the first Australian Aborigine to win an individual Olympic gold medal, it wasn't elation written all over Freeman's face.

It wasn't pride, it wasn't acknowledgement of the frenzied home crowd, in fact there wasn't even much joy.

It was relief.

She sat down in front of us, took off her shoes and, ever-so-briefly, just slumped.

Freeman now describes the pressure and build-up to her career-defining gold medal run as "unnatural".

She lit the flame to open the Sydney Olympic Games, she carried Australia to a rare track-and-field gold and she did it while speaking out as a young Aboriginal woman at a time when the world was focussed on Australia and all its beauty and its problems. And then, finally, it was over. Amid the circus and the expectations, she had done her job.

Her win in the 400 m to claim the gold is still my all-time top sporting moment — even though cheering wildly at the finish line was the closest I got to the event. I'm equally sure it won't be surpassed until one of my own kids takes to the field in their sport of choice and performs some amazing feat, like catching the ball, regardless of whether it is considered mediocre by any of the other one-eyed parents.

Until then, Freeman has shouldered my national pride and my gratitude for delivering on my Olympic dream -- and that of most of the other 20 million-odd Australians that day in September 2000.

That's really quite a load.

Four years later, Greece's 25-year-old Fani Halkia bore more than the pressure of an Olympic final when she stormed to 400 m hurdles gold in Athens.

Halkia's win was not just about an athlete overcoming an injured world-champion to claim a home-town victory. It was a redemption for Greece and 2004 host-city Athens, suffering from the scandal involving Greek sprint stars Kostas Kenderis and Ekaterina Thanou which blighted the start of the Games.

Touting itself as a clean Games — as it has become increasingly important for all Olympic hosts to do — Halkia's win deflected some of the heat after her teammates caused national shame by fleeing drug testers.

Such a responsibility brings us to Liu Xiang. Perhaps never has there been such Olympic expectation heaped on one slender frame.

On Thursday week, Liu will face the new world record holder and the fear of shattering the hopes of a billion people as he lines up to defend his Athens Olympic gold medal in the 110 m hurdles final.

It will be exciting. I already feel the nerves on Liu's behalf. Liu's win will be bigger than just a gold. Bigger than just an athlete winning at home. Without the gold medal, Liu has already been told his previous achievements will be worthless.

His win will be a proud moment for China. His win will prove, conclusively, that Asian athletes can take on and beat Western athletes in sports requiring strength, speed and power. It will prove that the Chinese can excel in sports other than ping-pong. And that one man – in a nation

*where individuals are rarely exalted above the masses – can bring a
moment of great pride and jubilation to more than 1.3 billion countrymen.*

*Try for a moment to imagine carrying that weight while you set about
your day job.*

The foreign media descending on Beijing soon experienced the type
of freedom the Chinese government was granting. They were not
happy. The International Federation of Journalists said the Beijing
Organising Committee reneged on previous media agreements,
effectively forcing foreign media organisations to acquire content
from Chinese state-owned broadcasters. The Chinese also brazenly
defied the International Olympic Committee by censoring the
Internet, especially websites relating to the Falun Gong, Amnesty
International and the Tiananmen Square massacre. Perhaps it was
down to the amount of time I had been in China and the media
control I had experienced through my job, but I wasn't at all
surprised by the move. Worryingly, I couldn't even feel outraged.
That was just China.

Despite all the protests and the argy bargy over media censorship,
the Games got under way with a spectacular Opening Ceremony.
The ceremony contained 29 fake firework footprint sequences and
featured a pretty nine-year-old lip-synching to another girl singing
'Hymn to the Motherland'. The original singer wasn't considered
'flawless' enough, so was dumped from the Ceremony limelight for
a prettier face. Again, I found I couldn't muster the indignation
expressed by so many foreign commentators that China would resort
to faking to project a 'perfect' image to the world. Of course they
would. It wouldn't happen at most other Olympics or in most other
countries, but this was China. I couldn't understand it or agree with

it, but I had accepted that China did things differently and a lot of our Western sensibilities about fairness and honesty did not apply. Maybe I'd been in a Chinese newsroom too long.

Strangely, despite all the build-up, the Olympic Games didn't impact in a bigger fashion on our daily lives in Shanghai. I'm not sure why I had expected them to. Perhaps it was that the Beijing Olympics were touted as being so much more than just a sporting event that I really felt that the Games' success would send immediate reverberations throughout China. Rather, I found the period of the Games for a foreigner living in China to be quite surreal. I would head into the office to work to be confronted by television screens full of ping-pong, badminton and gymnastics. My only contact with the Australian medal tally, especially in the first week when we were most likely to snare medals in the pool, was through the Internet. In the second week, even Jamaican Usain Bolt spectacularly shattering the world 100-metre record registered barely a blip in between the Chinese gymnastics, table tennis and tae kwon do.

China tallied 51 gold medals at the Beijing Games. Liu Xiang wasn't one of them. He withdrew in the first round of the event after sustaining an injury before the first hurdle and hobbling out of the Bird's Nest arena, leaving the crowd in stunned silence. The reaction in the office, though, was highly vocal and full of despair. I wondered if the opinion editor and editor in chief were taking note of staff members who were defying the Propaganda Department's ruling by displaying their devastation that China's great medal hope on the track had been eliminated.

As the Games ended, IOC president Jacques Rogge delivered a speech in which he said: 'Through these Games, the world learned more about China, and China learned more about the world.' For me, the lesson of the Beijing Olympics was that China did things the Chinese way. And, if they wanted a piece of China's success, it was up to everybody else to get onboard.

CHAPTER 18

HERE COMES HAIBO

'What did you think of the Olympic Games?'

It wasn't really a question. It was more an invitation. It was an opportunity for us to express our admiration and wonder at the show put on by China to impress the world at the Beijing Olympic Games. The Games were on the lips of just about every Chinese person we encountered, even weeks after the August 24 Closing Ceremony. Our Chinese friends were eager to hear what we thought and whether we had a new appreciation of China. If I thought the rest of the world may have looked upon China as staging a visually spectacular and highly organised yet flawed Games, there certainly wasn't a hint of concern among the Chinese. The Games showed

China's domination in the gold medal tally and just how well the Chinese could put on a show. The West may have criticised the Chinese along the themes of repression, control and censorship, but the Olympics were everything the Chinese hoped for.

I found that there was a very personal sense of achievement among the Chinese people regarding the Olympics. Within China there was not just pride. There was not just joy at China's great showing and record haul of gold medals. It was more like satisfaction. It was a sentiment that the world had finally seen just how great China was. And as a result, foreigners should be more respectful and hold the country in new esteem.

I told my inquisitors that I thought the Games looked spectacular. They did – the ceremonies were visually stunning and the facilities and organisation of the events were extraordinary. Without exception, the response to my reply was: 'Thank you very much.' It seemed a little odd. If anybody mentioned to me that they really enjoyed the Sydney Olympics, I doubt my response would ever have been to thank them, as if I personally had anything to do with it. But in China, the Games were that personal. And the satisfaction, joy and the pride that the Chinese felt was as intense as if they had won a gold medal themselves.

A friend of mine, Teena, told me her life had changed because of the Olympic Games. 'Before the Olympics, I would always tell people I am from Hong Kong. Now I say I am Chinese,' she said. She then sat back to enjoy my enthusiastic description of the Games and how I couldn't wait to visit the Olympic sites when I travelled to Beijing on a trip we were planning in October. She said she was very proud of her government and her people for putting on such a great show. 'I always knew it would be great, but I'm sure the world didn't expect it to be this good,' she said. Jane, another tell-it-like-it-is Chinese friend, was also keen to listen to our assessment of China's Olympics. Through our conversation I sensed real gratification that we were impressed. She too thanked us for our gushing response to the Olympics and prompted us to ensure we had grasped the full understanding of many of the cultural elements of the Opening and Closing Ceremonies.

The conversations, even with our most jaded and cynical Chinese friends, were a little like a test of our love for China. We were sensitive to the need to express our admiration, and happy to be effusive in our praise over the elements which genuinely wowed us. But we felt we couldn't mention the parts that didn't. In Australia, for whatever cultural reasons, we are quick to be critical and often save our most disparaging critiques for when we are assessing ourselves. When an event like the Olympics occurs, there is tremendous debate about what we are happy to celebrate and what makes us cringe about being Australian. And opinions remain divided even when the show is over – some having loved the production, others finding it an embarrassment. Among the Chinese it is different. I found universal acclaim for the Beijing Olympic ceremonies and a genuine incredulity when anyone expressed disapproval. When it emerged earlier, and was criticised in foreign media, that part of the elaborate fireworks show broadcast to the world in the Opening Ceremony was fake, the matter was explained away at the time by Chinese officials as not a deception, but rather a celebration of China's computer talents. The segment – 29 footprint-shaped fireworks running south to north across Beijing during the ceremony – were done digitally in 3-D computer graphics, including fake shake to simulate helicopter filming. The organisers seemingly did not see the need to hold an authentic ceremony when a computer generated one was more impressive. The producers' decision, just minutes before the ceremony started, to replace seven-year-old singer Yang Peiyi with lip-synching nine-year-old Lin Miaoke was also defended. The little girls were switched – at the orders of a member of the Chinese politburo – because Lin looked better on television than Yang who had buck teeth. 'The reason was for the nation's interest,' the ceremony's musical director Chen Qigang said. 'The child on camera should be flawless in image, internal feelings, and expression.'

I was careful not to bring the incidents up with our friends though I considered both totally dodgy and outrageous. I was at work when the stories came to light and faced the absolute bemusement of the Chinese journalists and editors that foreign media even considered the incidents newsworthy. Suggestions by some of the foreign experts that perhaps it was more important for the show to be authentic rather than fraudulently perfect in appearance were met with confused and unconvinced stares. None of us dared raise the scenario that by happily faking parts of the ceremony to showcase China's excellence to the world, it might raise questions over which other parts of China's Olympic Games performance might be fake or unfairly enhanced.

China won 51 gold medals at the Beijing Olympic Games, well ahead of its closest rival, the United States, with 36. Like most nations, the Chinese love a winner. But when it came to the losers, I was shocked by the swiftness with which one loser in particular was dumped from the Chinese consciousness. Liu Xiang, the 110 m hurdler, left Chinese fans deflated when he quit the Beijing Games after pulling up lame in one of the event's early heats. Liu was China's greatest hope for an athletics gold medal going in to the Games. The 25-year-old Shanghai athlete was such a focus in the lead-up to the Olympics that the Athens Olympic champion was awarded a 100 million-yuan (A$16 301 987) insurance policy against accidental injury by Chinese insurance giant Ping An Insurance Co. The day after Liu sensationally limped from the stadium, the *Shanghai Daily* ran a story on Liu's chances at winning an insurance payout. The head of the Chinese athletics team, Feng Shuyong, revealed Liu's injury was caused by a long-standing inflamed Achilles tendon in his right foot. Ping An issued a statement that the injury could not be considered an accidental injury so would not be covered by the policy. I thought the story was a terrific follow-up on the luckless hurdler. But Liu Xiang did not win gold for China. He was no longer of any interest. The story was buried back in the paper's business section.

The Chinese win-at-all-costs outlook was by no means unique. But thinking about the nation's yearning for glory and need to win spectacularly in Beijing – often regardless of the cost to individuals – reminded me that my Shanghai friends never failed to mention in our Olympic discussions that the Games were about so much more than sport. They said the Beijing Olympics needed to introduce new China to the world and enliven the nation's standing internationally. It was about competing for attention on the world stage. China was always about competition. Helping me understand for the first time the depth of competitiveness even within China, they then said it would be up to Shanghai to do an even better job than Beijing when they grabbed the international spotlight for Shanghai World Expo 2010. 'Just wait until Shanghai shows what we can do,' they said. And, sure enough, one day after the Beijing Olympic Closing Ceremony, Shanghai was awash with blobby blue Haibos, the Shanghai World Expo 2010 mascot.

It was not long after Haibo began dominating the Shanghai landscape, popping up randomly in parks, in office foyers, on building sites and swathes of billboards and hoardings, that we headed to Beijing.

We decided to brave the late September Golden Week transport crush and visit the Chinese capital in the hope it would still be a city clinging to its Olympic success in a kind of satisfied trance. We thought it would be a nice juxtaposition to the feverish preparations of pre-Expo Shanghai. We were warned against such folly by our expat friends who tried to convince us that there was no joy to be had in travelling within China in Golden Week, but we headed off regardless. It appeared millions of Chinese – and at least a few thousand foreigners – had the same idea.

And they were all there at our must-see destinations. We braved the crowds to visit the Forbidden City carrying the children on our shoulders through the Meridian Gate. We flowed with the tide of sightseers around the beauty of the Summer Palace. We carted the children into Tiananmen Square, which was the only place we found the crowds too overwhelming. Instead went and got lost wandering through the park surrounding the stunning fifteenth-century-built Temple of Heaven, while following elderly locals flying their magnificent kites shaped like eagles. We found the city a breath of fresh air as we took leisurely walks through *hutong*, the traditional alleys, of the capital. It felt ridiculous to say it out loud, but in a city of more than 16 million people – plus the influx of travellers for Golden Week – Beijing felt more relaxed and plain easier than Shanghai. The air was relatively clean, the people were friendly and the food was magnificent – which was fortunate given we endured more than a two-hour wait with hungry children to satisfy their mother's desire for a seat at the famous Quanjude Roast Duck Restaurant just off Wangfujing Dajie (street). The restaurant chain has been serving up its internationally renowned Peking duck since 1864 and our duck was so delicious it was almost worth the wait. But the kids only ate dumplings.

We chatted with taxi drivers who had been ordered to learn English before the Olympics and were still keen to demonstrate their prowess. It may have been weeks since the Olympics had ended, but when we visited the Games Park and its spectacular Bird's Nest National Stadium and the Water Cube or National Aquatic Centre, we were among thousands who were overjoyed just to be wandering at night outside the closed buildings.

And we went to the Great Wall of China. On China's National Day, October 1, the Great Wall at Mutianyu couldn't have been more crowded, nor more breath-taking. It was the culmination of a wonderful week in Beijing. It was a week that allowed us to see the Chinese capital still in its best possible light before we headed back to Shanghai, Haibo and mounting Expo fever – though of course it may have been that I was oblivious to anything negative in my surrounds and flushed with general goodwill to all Beijingers, indeed all Chinese, by being able to call myself Smarty's fiancée.

CHAPTER 19

MILKING A SCANDAL

We thought we were so clever. It may have taken about eight months of living in Shanghai, but we finally found a rare stash of edible Shanghai bread. It was called Fresh Nature Bread and it was white and soft and stayed unnaturally fresh for about a week. I was sure it couldn't be good for us, but we ate it anyway because the kids loved it and I figured it was better to give them a sandwich as a treat than biscuits or sweets. If I called into the local 24-hour Lawson market on Xikang Lu on the way home between midnight and 1 a.m., I usually caught the delivery guys. I liked buying my bread at the Lawson right off the truck for a couple of reasons: I got the only two eight-slice loaves of Fresh Nature Bread the staff put out on the shelves each day, and the doors to the store were open to allow the deliveries in, which meant I was not overwhelmed by cigarette smoke while trying to buy food.

The city in summer was extremely hot and sticky and even in the early hours of the morning, the smoke in confined spaces like food stores hung at the entrance like a muslin veil, wafting back only to the swing of the front doors or the irregular gasps of a shuddering air conditioner. In the middle of the day the Chinese shopkeepers might obey the crack down on smoking in public places that was a hangover from the recent Olympics, but in the middle of the night it was another story. As I headed up Xikang Lu, I passed men in their pyjamas taking their dogs for a midnight walk and girls in very short dresses just walking. There was also a couple who set up a little fried noodle stand about midnight to catch late night local snack-seekers and expat men stumbling out of the nearby Big Bamboo sports bar. At the foggy Lawson, one of Shanghai's mini-mart chains, I could not only buy bread but Nelson's favourite nori seaweed sheets and our milk of choice. The milk we liked, after sampling about a dozen on offer, was produced by the Chinese Bright dairy company and came in a white cardboard container. We couldn't work out the name of the milk because there was no English on the packaging, which was why I'd often mistakenly come home with litre containers of runny yoghurt instead of milk when the Lawson had sold out of our milk-in-a-white-box. The milk had the flavour of Chinese dairy, which was thinner and sweeter than we were accustomed to in Australia. The milk-in-a-white-box, though, was thicker than most other brands we'd tasted and had a nice creamy layer on top that reminded me a little of many years ago when milk at home was delivered in bottles and how my dad would always blame my brother for stealing the much-sought-after top layer of cream even though we could actually see the tell-tale white milk moustache atop Dad's lip.

The kids had been on a feeding frenzy through much of the summer and had shaken off their recurring bouts of illness to start growing like bamboo. At the height of summer in July, Milly celebrated her fourth birthday. We had a party at the One Park Avenue playground with her friends who weren't part of the annual Shanghai expat mass summer exodus.

It was in summer that I truly began to understand the bewildered looks our family attracted when we mentioned that we had moved to Shanghai from our home in Australia barely two minutes from the beach. And that we had no intention of going home at all during the summer (never mind that it was actually mid-winter in Australia at the time and that the temperatures in our neck of the woods plummeted to what we considered a chilly 10 degrees Celsius at night).

The summer heat in Shanghai seemed never-ending. And, again, we'd had to adapt.

Just like locals, we'd gone to strange lengths to find respite from the heat. On even short walks we began crossing the street numerous times to catch the shade of buildings, awnings, umbrellas, trees, even street stalls offering the knick-knacks I was normally at great pains to steer the kids away from.

We'd become water-logged spending time in the bath and the One Park Avenue pool to stay cool. And we'd taken to afternoon sleeps because the children, and their mother, could only sap up so much heat and humidity in one morning and eventually had to succumb to the lure of cool, crisp sheets and an afternoon of heat-free hanging out.

The Shanghai summer taught us that there was not much in the way of snacks that couldn't be frozen. Milly, going through a period of vegetable refusal, offered me a deal. She said she would eat her broccoli if I made it into an ice block. And, as though a four-year-old could understand the notion of saving face, once I'd agreed to her request, she even proceeded to eat it (argh!).

The summer became a time of bonding with friends as we sought shelter from the heat in each other's houses. It was also a chance to explore indoor attractions we might not normally have included on our itinerary – a cheap favourite was the dusty dinosaurs of the Shanghai Natural History Museum on Yan'an Dong Lu which was so delightfully run down it felt like we were explorers discovering a long-ago hidden tomb of bones, mummies and grotesque animal carcases each time we visited.

We understood why so many of our expat friends disappeared to cooler climes or returned home for the duration of the summer. But it was without complaint that we 'endured' staying behind in Shanghai.

At Milly's birthday party, the expat and local children who attended all looked like they were going to melt after running around in the sweltering late afternoon heat. Unfortunately the extremely expensive store-bought chocolate cake featuring an iced depiction of Disney's Ariel the Little Mermaid did. We also staged a BBQ, although a local government crackdown on meat product manufacturing meant there was not a sausage to be had in Shanghai.

We had to make do with my kids' favourite honey and soy-marinated Chinese chicken wings.

Despite so many months in Shanghai, Milly had still not taken to Chinese cuisine and her diet, which dictated what the rest of our household ate when we were at home, consisted of egg whites – neither child would eat egg yolks – with Fresh Nature toast for breakfast, kindy lunch, followed by another lunch with fruit and cheese at home, and my marinated chicken wings or pasta variations for dinner. *Ayi* Tina also cooked for us at least one night a week and showed up with surprise ingredients including mystery live fish, lotus root, tofu and Chinese vegetables that I had to call by their Chinese names as I had never seen them before. Both children would only drink water or milk, which helped streamline the shopping.

I'd finally got the weekly grocery shopping organised. It took six months to get that sorted. In China it's very difficult to source quality products that are foreign to Chinese cooking. It's a very rare occurrence to be able to buy everything for a meal from a single shop. And it's often the case that a store that stocks a much-sought after item one week, will not carry it again for months. The upside of shopping in China though is that once you have found what you're after, you can get almost anything delivered for free. A quick call to the One Park Avenue management saw bottled water delivered to my door. It took a lot of patience and not-so-patient cursing of their website, but I also arranged a weekly delivery of items such as nappies, toothpaste and toilet paper from the French supermarket chain Carrefour. As well as the deliveries, I would dive into my favourite local wet market and fruit and vegetable shops most days and pop into the Lawson nightly in search of Fresh Nature

Bread and milk-in-a-white-box. I felt I'd finally conquered what many would consider the normally simple task of buying food and groceries and had begun feeling confident about what I was feeding the family, even if I had restricted our diet quite significantly compared to the range of meals I prepared back in Australia. Despite the gruesome thought of them being grown in night soil, I felt most assured making meals based on local vegetables. I saved up to occasionally buy imported Australian lamb, but purchased local pork and chicken. The Chinese favour the flavour of chicken near the bone, so I could get chicken breast fillets really cheaply at two for about 8 yuan (A$1.30), while chicken wings cost about the same for a pack of eight. Many of the expat mums I spoke to wouldn't touch local chicken. I almost didn't want to find out why because removing chicken from the roster would create a huge hole in the family's already limited weekly menu. And I'd been so careful in reaction to the many health scares related to Chinese products – lead paint in toy trains, toothpaste containing the toxic chemicals found in antifreeze and tainted pet food responsible for killing cats and dogs across the United States – that I was starting to feel food caution fatigue. Surely we would have been alerted if there was a problem with something so widely consumed as chicken.

I should never have been so trusting. On September 11, the *Oriental Morning Post* carried a story that shattered our fragile confidence. We could no longer believe anything was safe in China. The paper blew the whistle on the dairy corporation, Sanlu Group, alleging the company had been producing milk powder laced with melamine. Melamine is a tasteless white powder used in the manufacture of plastic that can artificially inflate the protein readings in milk products. When raw milk is diluted with water or other agents the amount of protein drops, but melamine can fool the tests. It raises the appearance or markers of protein but not the actual level. Melamine, when consumed, can be toxic to the kidneys. In high enough doses it can kill babies. Sanlu were adding melamine to baby formula.

The Chinese government confirmed the contamination on September 15, when the General Administration of Quality Supervision, Inspection and Quarantine (AQSIQ) issued a public warning on Sanlu milk powder. AQSIQ said tests revealed there was melamine in 22 different dairy products sold in China. The story quickly accelerated to a national disaster. Reports of the number of babies suffering kidney problems and being taken to hospitals across the country multiplied daily until thousands were receiving medical treatment. At least four babies died. After initially thinking the contamination was just in baby formula, we were shocked to discover it was also in regular milk. We immediately threw away all our milk. Some lovely homemade ice-cream sent over by a friend ended up in the bin as well. There was no point thinking any milk product would have been spared the contamination. We'd learned during our time in China that things were generally much worse than we'd been led to believe.

Apart from Sanlu Group products, Bright, Yili and Mengniu milk and yoghurt were found to be contaminated. The authorities told us that all baby formula, milk and other dairy products laced with the melamine had been removed from the shelves. At Shanghai's markets, dairy cases and shelves were bare of the local products as well as all brands of imported longlife milk. Among expats especially there had been panic buying of imported milk. On Internet chat rooms parents were urging other families not to hoard milk so others could access the imported supply. I couldn't find any milk I thought was safe and had to explain to the kids that they could only have water to drink and that they would be going without cheese and butter for a while. I didn't want to scare them by telling them milk might be poisonous, so I went with a tale that China had run out. I overheard Milly telling Nelson that night that all the cows must be sleeping, but they'd wake up one day and we could all have milk again. It would be nice if reasons other than human avarice were to blame for the milk ban.

Dairy is not a regular component of the Chinese diet, though many Chinese parents feed their babies formula. The reaction by the Chinese public to the scandal seemed to me to be very reserved. While I was involved in daily discussions with expat friends outraged at the crisis, many Chinese – especially those who did not have children – appeared detached. In a vox pop, or street interviews, with Shanghai residents by the *Shanghai Daily*, only two of five locals whose comments were published in the paper were worried about the contamination. The remainder expressed confidence the government had the problem under control.

The government didn't. Hong Kong's Centre for Food Safety announced it had found melamine in a sample of Lotte Cream Cheese Cake made in China. It also found melamine in the company's Koala's March chocolate and strawberry cream cookies. Soon there was a wave of recalls. Chinese-made White Rabbit candies were recalled after testing positive in both New Zealand and Australia for melamine. Cadbury recalled its Cadbury éclairs. A vegetable formula cereal produced by Heinz and a steamed potato wasabi produced by Silang were also pulled from shelves. At work one night I received a text message from a friend at the Australian consulate in Shanghai containing a list of products including popular chocolates, biscuits, crackers, cakes and sweets found to contain melamine. It said Cadbury dairy milk chocolate, cookies, Snickers bars, M&Ms and KitKats had been deemed unsafe. Although the information was obviously available to officials from Australia, such a list hadn't appeared in the Chinese newspaper. Rather, the *Shanghai Daily* news pages had been filled with the government's containment of the problem. I'd learned my lesson about questioning what was included in the paper and what was left out. Instead, I emailed and texted the list to my friends and said I hoped they weren't relying on the State-run media for information.

By late September, it seemed the crisis was beginning to subside. The government officially gave milk products the all clear. AQSIQ said it had tested 2826 batches of milk produced after the government went public with the scandal and found none were tainted with the industrial chemical. By October 11, it said tests had also cleared 460 batches of baby formula from 50 brands and 576 batches of other milk powder from 133 brands produced after September 14. China's famous White Rabbit candy, produced in Shanghai, was also cleared to go back on sale.

The contamination scandal claimed the lives of six infants. More than 294 000 babies became sick in China after consuming melamine. The scandal affected products exported and consumed in countries around the world. We thought the worst had passed.

But there was more to come. Melamine was also in eggs. Melamine was found in eggs sold by four Chinese brands as well as in animal feed in farms around the country. The melamine was added to feed given to chickens that subsequently laid contaminated eggs. We had to throw out all our eggs. I began feeling sick with worry that the kids may have consumed enough melamine to fall ill. They had been going through at least a litre of milk a day up until the crisis and regularly had eggs for breakfast, often three or four egg whites at a time. All I could do was watch them closely for signs of illness and double check everything going into their mouths.

It was also suggested melamine had been added to feed for poultry, cows, sheep, pigs and fish. Shanghai authorities announced they were carrying out checks on feed used in the fisheries industry due to fears the food scandal had spread to seafood. We asked *ayi* Tina to stop buying fish to cook for dinner. I cut local meat from our diet along with eggs and milk. Instead, I happily paid the inflated prices for imported meat, considering the A$10 for two lamb chops or $30 for a kilo of beef mince worth it to keep the family safe.

The food contamination crisis was difficult for authorities to deal with. The government promised to overhaul its food safety regulatory authorities and severely punish those responsible for the contamination. But Chinese babies had died and thousands more were seriously ill. It felt like authorities weren't doing enough. Still, there was an even more sinister element to the scandal. It soon emerged that it could have been stopped months earlier. At best it could be said a lack of transparency in China's political system and the tight control of information within the country hampered the effectiveness of the nation's regulatory authorities. At worst, it was a massive cover up, suspected of being perpetrated so China didn't suffer the embarrassment of a food contamination scandal while the world spotlight was on the country for the Beijing Olympic Games.

The *New York Times* detailed claims that parents who tried to act as whistleblowers were fobbed off or ignored by authorities and Chinese journalists were blocked by censorship rules banning coverage of politically touchy subjects in the lead-up to the Olympics. The American newspaper said AQSIQ was aware there was contaminated milk on the market as early as June – more than three months before the scandal became public. It said a mother from Hunan Province had written a series of letters to Sanlu and AQSIQ over an increasing number of infants developing kidney stones. 'Urgent! Urgent! Urgent!' she wrote. 'Please investigate whether the formula does have problems, or more babies will get sick.' Her pleas were ignored by the food safety body.

A reporter at the *Southern Weekly*, one of China's few independent publications, told *Shanghai Daily* intern Ananth Krishnan for an investigative piece he wrote for the Indian media, that the newspaper had come under 'serious pressure' after reporting in July that infants had started falling ill in Jiangsu province after consuming Sanlu milk. A *Southern Weekly* editor, Fu Jianfeng, wrote in his blog on September 14. 'As a news editor, I was very concerned. I had realised that this was a huge public disaster, but I could not send out my reporters …We couldn't do any investigation on an issue like this, at that time, in order to be harmonious,' he wrote. In July, another newspaper based in Nanjing reported that fifteen sick infants in a two-month period had been taken to the city's children's hospital. The newspaper did not mention the source of the poisoning, but rather cryptically urged readers to keep babies away from children's milk products and 'breast-feed their children more'. In July, cases of milk poisoning were also being reported in Beijing, Xian and in the provinces of Anhui and Hubei. But none of the cases were addressed by the authorities as clusters that needed to be investigated.

On August 2, still more than a month before the government warned the public to stop drinking milk and feeding their babies formula laced with toxin, executives of the New Zealand dairy giant Fonterra were informed of the problem. Sanlu is a joint venture with Fonterra which owns a 43 per cent share of the company and has three members on the board. Fonterra's executives said their representatives pushed for a public recall, but were overruled by the rest of the board. One official said the company decided 'to work inside the Chinese system', meaning with Sanlu management and local authorities. The problem was finally exposed in September just after the New Zealand government, following discussions with Fonterra executives, contacted authorities in Beijing.

Beijing officials continued to say they knew nothing about the scandal until September. Despite evidence of warnings and even a Fonterra spokesman who went on the record to suggest the central government knew in August, the Chinese government denied any delay or cover up. The Chinese public were not convinced. What started as confidence the government was doing all it could ended as a roar of discontent. Among the expat community there was outrage, heightened by the frustration there was no avenue for us to complain and no recourse for us against a government that treated its people in such a fashion. Domestically, the government also received uncommonly harsh criticism from furious parents and stinging rebukes from hundreds of thousands of netizens. Even state-owned newspapers joined the unusually vocal criticism of the government's handling of the scandal. It was an issue that went to the heart of the Chinese people's trust in government. If the authorities knew and did nothing, they helped babies die.

But, like a tightly choreographed dance, the furore peaked then quickly abated. The public had its chance to blow off steam and the government quickly won back control. Soon the dominant stories in the newspapers returned to parents and members of the public expressing their appreciation for the government's swift and severe reaction. I detected that Chinese friends of mine didn't engage when the subject of the government culpability in the milk scandal was brought up, even though their families were still off local dairy. I dropped the subject entirely when Diane, a mum who I considered my wisest and most worldly Chinese pal, responded with a wearied shrug.

My expat friends and I, though, weren't so forgiving. Many of my friends said they couldn't understand how locals could accept the way they had been treated. Some said they'd begun noticing in their dealings with Chinese mums how many had even begun praising the government for not alerting the public earlier because it would only have caused mass panic. They said some of their Chinese friends told them they understood how important avoiding a scandal during the Olympics was to protecting China's image. I decided there was no point raising an argument when I heard this sort of thinking. My stance on cover ups and complicity in killing babies was too far away from this sort of trust in a wise and benevolent government for there ever to be any common ground in such a discussion. I made certain to keep such thoughts contained at work. And, no doubt like mothers throughout China, I was too occupied trying to ensure my family were consuming non-toxic meals to get caught up in an ultimately futile squabble over government responsibility in such a scandal. I chalked my attitude up to another change in me that had come with living in China. I couldn't imagine that I'd not complain just because I thought my protests might be ineffectual and that I'd accept I could never change things were I living in a country like Australia.

The Chinese government did act to try to restore public confidence in its food safety system. It quickly released a new list of 17 illegal food additives including substances commonly used in industrial dyes, insecticides and drain cleaners. The list was China's first banned additives register. On it was boric acid, normally used as an insecticide, which was being mixed with noodles and meatballs to increase elasticity. Also forbidden was industrial formaldehyde and lye, used in making soap and drain cleaner and added to water used to soak some types of dried seafood to make the products appear fresher. The list included various industrial dyes that were being added to improve the appearance of food products ranging from chilli powder to tea to cooked meats. An addictive substance made from the poppy plant and related to opium which could be used as a painkiller was also banned. The substance was often used in hot pot, a popular Chinese dish where meat, vegetables and tofu are cooked at the table. Also listed was Sudan red, a cancer-causing industrial dye used to colour egg yolks. And, of course, melamine.

The people responsible for the Sanlu contamination were also identified and punished.

Xinhua reported Tian Wenhua, the 66-year-old general manager and chairwoman of Sanlu Group was sentenced to life and fined 24.7 million yuan (A$4.2m). She pleaded guilty to producing and selling fake or substandard milk. Sanlu's former deputy general managers, Wang Yuliang and Hang Zhiqi, were fined and sentenced to fifteen and eight years. Wu Jusheng, a former executive heading Sanlu's milk division, was sentenced to five years in prison.

Two men, Zhang Yujun and Geng Jinping, were executed. Xinhua said Zhang Yujun was convicted of endangering public safety by dangerous means for selling more than 770 tonnes of the tainted milk powder. Xinhua said Geng Jinping was convicted of supplying milk containing melamine to Sanlu and other dairies.

Xinhua said fourteen others involved in the scandal were punished. The punishments were swift and sharp and successfully focused lingering anger, especially among parents of the affected children, on a small group of perpetrators.

For some parents it wasn't enough. Some launched legal action for compensation. In an open letter published in December, Sanlu and 21 other dairy companies offered 200 000 yuan (A$32 603) each to families whose children died and 30 000 yuan (A$4890) for serious illnesses such as kidney stones and acute kidney failure. They also offered 2000 yuan (A$326) for victims in less severe cases. Some parents took the money. Others went to court. There seemed to be a lot of fight in a lot of parents. I wondered how the parents would ever recover knowing they poisoned their babies by feeding them the formula they needed to grow and survive. What would they ever be able to trust? What amount of compensation could be enough for the trauma those families had been through?

Sanlu Group went bankrupt. Beijing Sanyuan Foods Co, the only
listed company to sell melamine-free products during the dairy
scandal, said its net profit in 2008 jumped 87.2 per cent from a year
earlier – to around 40.75 million yuan (A$6.64 million). Exports of
China's dairy products dropped 10.4 per cent to 121 000 tonnes in
2008. The General Administration of Customs astutely put the
decline down to shrinking demand from overseas. Conversely,
imports were up. The country imported 351 000 tonnes of dairy
products at a cost of US$860 million, a 17.4 per cent rise in volume
on the previous year.

The scandal and its aftermath made us assess again everything we
were putting into our mouths in China. We felt there was no longer
room for the attitude that we should sample strange local food so
we could go home and tell the anecdotes. This was our real life and I
was devastated that after being so careful to always give the kids a
well-balanced diet, we may have been unwittingly feeding our
children food that could have caused real damage. Shopping for food
again became as difficult and time consuming as it was when we first
moved to China. I managed to source some milk imported from
Japan and another batch regularly available from New Zealand. I
found eggs that also came from Japan, cheese from New Zealand,
pasta from Italy and meat from Australia. I also checked everything I
bought locally to ensure it did not contain milk products or high
MSG content. I even contemplated buying imported noodles. All the
imported produce caused my weekly grocery shopping bill to shoot
up to more than I would pay in a week in Australia. I returned to
spending chunks of the day seeking out food for dinner and washing,
soaking, boiling and peeling fresh produce. I did not open a tin or a

packet until *ayi* Tina assured me there was no risk from the food. I felt the responsibility was entirely on me and that I could not trust food to be safe just because it had supposedly passed quality tests and made it on to market shelves.

But I did continue to pop into the Lawson on the way home each night in search of one thing that remained a staple in our diets – Fresh Nature Bread. That was until a story crossed my desk at the *Shanghai Daily* in late November. It said authorities in China were considering banning the use of a flour whitener widely used in China. Rice might be the grain favoured in the south, but flour is the staple of northern China and used to make noodles, dumplings, pancakes and steamed buns. And, of course, bread. Authorities said they were investigating the use of benzoyl peroxide – the active ingredient in many acne creams that was also used to bleach flour. After contaminated milk, and eggs, I wondered if we really could endure a health scare over noodles, dumplings and bread.

CHAPTER 20

A DUMPLING FOR EVERY OCCASION

The Chinese are obsessed with food. Asking if someone had eaten or was hungry was part of an everyday greeting. Chinese people also tended to eat anywhere, at any time. Restaurants filled throughout the day, were packed in the early evening and were still full late at night. And local people seemed to love a snack. Food was available not only in restaurants and cafés, but from street vendors, mobile snack carts and back-of-the-bicycle peddlers. I met so many people who never cooked at home, including the Chinese mother of one of Milly's kindergarten friends who asked me where we took breakfast. She was shocked to learn I made the kids' breakfast myself.

Food in Shanghai, from the moment we arrived, had also been one of my obsessions. It was very sad that contamination and mistrust meant we'd had to add a whole new dimension of suspicion to the fun and challenge of eating. There had been twin delights in the hunt for good food in the city. One had been the surprise of the non-Chinese cuisine. While there were famous top end restaurants equal to any in the world, it had actually been more fun, and bizarrely more satisfying, finding a Chinese restaurant that could make a good hamburger. My colleagues and I often indulged in the hit-and-miss pastime of ordering non-Chinese food in to the office at night. It was usually quite entertaining. If someone stumbled upon a decent hamburger, it would be the subject of inspection and talked about for weeks. The magnitude of such a discovery meant that we would all order it, only for the famed burger to invariably fail to live up to expectations and send someone scurrying off to the bathroom. And that's how yet another restaurant would get culled from our ordering list.

It's more than faintly ridiculous that we even tried to find a great hamburger in Shanghai. But I was confronted by an even more profound 'something just doesn't belong' sensation when I stumbled across two Australian expat enterprises in the city making and selling meat pies. I very rarely eat a meat pie in Australia, but found myself salivating at the thought of it in China. It actually felt quite wrong to be in Shanghai eating a pie. So I didn't. I got the pie company to deliver one of their pavlovas to my door instead. Then, just to remind me I really was in China, I spent an entire day searching for whipping cream. I failed and ended up having to offer dinner guests, intrigued by my offer of a fabulous pavlova after dinner treat, dry meringue and fruit.

The bigger gastronomic thrill in Shanghai was eating at local restaurants. As I worked nights and couldn't leave the office, I tended to let Smarty do the feasting around town in his lunch break so he could provide recommendations that might suit the family for the two nights a week we had together. We agreed early after our arrival in China that I couldn't afford to get sick as it would throw the whole family into disarray. Smarty's role had therefore also been part restaurant guinea pig. He had ended up in the doctor's office on a saline drip twice from stomach bugs, but had saved the family from eating at restaurants that might have had us all laid up. I was disappointed I hadn't been able to indulge in Shanghai's array of culinary offerings, and street food in particular, with as much gusto as I may have in my pre-children days. But I accepted that I couldn't take time out from caring for the kids because I'd eaten something dodgy and I certainly wasn't prepared to subject them to something that could make them ill. I had to find the balance between being adventurous and trying all the new, wonderful and weird food available, and being a great big chicken.

Ordering in local Chinese restaurants was often extremely difficult. Menus were rarely in English and most contained pages and pages of options. We'd sit down to dinner never knowing how many dishes to order, or often what we'd actually ordered. But we continued to try and sampled many of the restaurants in our neighbourhood. It wasn't easy as restaurants that were there one week could very quickly be torn down and replaced by a different one the next. But we found some favourites. And we learned enough to declare we were no fans of Shanghai cuisine. In my experience Shanghai cuisine seemed to involve taking anything remotely edible and drowning it in broth. The dishes that weren't swimming in broth were doused heavily in oil and all were quite sweet.

Almost all dishes can be cooked in the Shanghai style known as *hongshao* – braised with oil, soy sauce and sugar – and end up looking dark red or brown, even the fish. Shanghai's snacks are probably more renowned. They fall into categories depending on whether they're steamed, boiled, fried or baked. The snacks were available throughout the day – from mystery balls on a stick that people pulled from simmering pots of water in corner stores, to eggs of various shades of grey, to strange sweet snacks like ice-creams designed to look like carrots. The best snacks seemed to be on offer in the mornings and were eaten for breakfast.

Among traditional Shanghainese families, breakfast is often eaten at home. It's usually rice stewed with water, called *paofan*, with salted vegetables, *xiancai*. Dim sum is also popular for breakfast in Shanghai, including *dabing*, large flatbread, *youtiao*, deep-fried twisted dough sticks, *doujiang*, soybean milk, and *cifangao*, glutinous rice cake. The breakfast staples are referred to as the 'Four Great King Kongs' as they are the most traditional and popular breakfast foods among locals. Another dim sum I came across and really quite liked was *xiekehuang* pancake, or crab shell cakes, which were a baked spring onion-stuffed sesame biscuit. I was told by Chinese friends they were called crab shell cakes, not because they contained the famous dumpling filler of 'fried ovary and digestive glands of a crab', but because they look like a boiled crab shell and the name means crab shell in Chinese. There was a savoury and a sweet version of the pancake. The savoury stuffing was made of green onion, fresh pork, crab powder and shrimp shells. The sweet stuffing was made of sugar, rose, sweet bean paste and Chinese date mud. The savoury option was my favourite, although the ones I tasted were a little dry.

Soup is particularly big in Shanghai. In China, soup is generally taken at the end of the meal. It's an essential and locals consider a meal incomplete without it. As with most Chinese cuisine, soup isn't just about what tastes good. There's an entire culture built around the health benefits of soup. I have to confess that I don't like soup. Any soup. Not even wonton soup, *xiao huntun*. I struggled the entire year with the Chinese soup culture.

There are three kinds of soups in Chinese cuisine and they're set apart by the method in which they are cooked. There is boiled soup (*guntang*), double-boiled soup (*duntang* or *weitang*) and simmered soup (*baotang*). *Guntang* is the quickest to prepare and the most popular homemade soup in Shanghai. Tomato and egg soup is probably the most famous *guntang*. I don't know if it has any particular healing properties, though many other soups do. The *Shanghai Daily* explained that double-boiled chicken soup with ginseng was said to help hair retain its blackness, aid digestion and sooth the nerves. Double-boiled frog soup was meant to improve eyesight, reinforce the blood and energy (qi) and improve the skin. Turtle with *longan* and *gou qi* berries reinforced Yin energy, improved eyesight and helped the spleen function, while double-boiled pigeon with yams and *gou qi* benefitted the liver, spleen and kidneys and reinforced qi. Pig foot soup was supposed to be so good for the skin it was said to be one of the secret weapons of a Chinese woman's beauty. While the soups all sounded extremely beneficial, I was never tempted.

Our favourite Chinese meal of the week was invariably made by *ayi* Tina. She was from Nanjing and didn't cook in the Shanghai style. Her cooking seemed straightforward, yet she could even make basic pork and bamboo shoots delicious. She assured me MSG was not one of her main ingredients, but I remained baffled as to how she got everything to taste so good. The children – even Milly – always enjoyed her cooking and both would hop into tofu and rice and vegetables they would never touch if I were to make it for them. I was always really disappointed I had to go to work and couldn't stay at home for dinner on the nights Tina cooked.

As I had to go to work, I found some regular dishes I was happy to order at restaurants close to the office when I just couldn't handle another foray into the offerings of Shanghai's Western food outlets. The restaurants had no English names, nor did the dishes. I made quite a habit of popping over to a restaurant Smarty and I nicknamed 'The Bucket' at 724 Weihai Lu and ordering their dish pictured at the top right of their in-store promotional poster. We called the restaurant The Bucket because the takeaway came in a container about the size of a child's small sandcastle bucket. It was always pretty good value – my rice with stir-fried beef and onions was the most expensive on the menu at 16 yuan (A$2.60). Every dish was prepared on the spot which gave me a few spare minutes to browse the shop full of knock-off DVDs at 714 Weihai Lu, which in our experience had quite good quality fakes. If I wasn't in the mood for The Bucket and had the chance to leave the office for more than five minutes, I headed down to 'The Knuckle', another restaurant that had no official English name, at 834 Weihai Lu. Its pork knuckle and rice was always popular. I preferred the spiced eggplant to the knuckle dish, though I'm not sure anyone should eat something with that much oil, even if it tasted as good as this did.

On my nights off, we regularly went to one of our two favourite Chinese restaurants. 'The Local' at the corner of Beijing Xie Lu and Xinzha Lu came with an English menu and a variety that suited all members of the family. It offered a particularly good spicy prawn dish, dumplings and sizzling beef for Nelson, and bland noodles we told Milly were actually spaghetti. We never failed to be delighted that the bill for a family meal that we couldn't finish came in at under 80 yuan (A$13). Our favourite restaurant, however, was 'The Uygur Joint' on the corner of Wuding Lu and Xikang Lu, which had the big *tono* or oven for baking bread outside. The food of the people from Xinjiang Uygur Autonomous Region in far western China is spicy and based largely on lamb and wheat. We passed on most of the noodle dishes for the flat breads and lamb, from kebabs to dumplings to large chunks of a whole roasted animal. The food was great and the ambience even better. As soon as the restaurant had a few diners settled, the owner would break out in song and soon had diners on their feet joining in and dancing. The kids especially enjoyed the dancing girl who performed most nights. Her sensual, veiled dancing manoeuvres lost a little of their mysterious appeal however when there were two tiny blonde children dancing along with her and latching on to her floaty scarves. But the locals seemed to love it anyway.

When not eating out in Shanghai, shopping for food was quite the task. Some of my expat friends never shopped for food or cooked. It might have saved a massive amount of trouble and effort, but it bypassed a whole avenue of insight and experience of the Chinese culture.

When we first arrived and I was trying to get my bearings and find familiar food, I was thrilled to find an outlet of the British retail chain Tesco. I wandered through the clothing and electrical departments feeling quite relaxed and happy in such familiar shopping surrounds. Then I hit the fresh food level. Great mounds of chicken feet and other meat cuts were piled high on 'sale' tables. Shoppers were picking up and tossing aside the raw meats with their bare hands before selecting the preferred piece from the heap. Other meats were laid out behind a glass cabinet on bloodied boards so staff members could cut customers a slice with giant cleavers. Even if I were prepared to risk buying a piece of meat like this, I couldn't have. I couldn't identify any of the beasts from whence the cuts came, except of course chicken. I have to admit I prefer my meat to come portioned, labelled and wrapped in plastic. The kids always enjoyed going to Tesco, if only for the seafood section. Giant tanks filled with swimming, and some floating, fish sat in the middle of the supermarket aisle. Water sloshed all over the floor as shoppers used little nets to catch their fish and take it flipping and flopping in a plastic bag to the checkout. The kids thought the whole process was terrific and I always had to physically pick them up and place them complaining and wet with fish water and eel slime into the trolley when I was ready to leave. I usually extracted them from the fish area after becoming bamboozled by the egg section. In the egg section, there were at least 20 different egg types to choose from. I couldn't understand any of the writing so always had to rifle through to find one with a picture of chickens on the pack. It made me more appreciative of Bernie's offering of eggs in the fridge with a chicken on the pack when we first arrived.

Tesco, like other large Western shops in Shanghai, still retains much of its big supermarket chain essence. The local wet market is a whole other experience. There are about 900 wet markets in Shanghai. The markets are full of fresh vegetables, live fish and freshly butchered meat. Our closest wet market was at 520 Xikang Lu. Compared to some others I'd visited it was clean and didn't smell too bad. I still cut back on my visits to the market in summer when the aromas were all a bit more intense. On first entering the market it could be overwhelming, especially if you were there to buy, not just to look. The markets are stocked by farmers from surrounding areas such as Shanghai's Nanhui and Songjiang districts and neighbouring Chongming County. Vegetables, fruit, fresh meat and live seafood made up the bulk of the market's offerings. There were eels being caught, fish being gutted, crabs being collected, and an endless supply of turtles. There were whole displays of pig snouts, eyeballs, ears, feet and tongues, and lots of livers, hearts and other internal organs. In the dried food section there were all sorts of beans, fungi, different varieties of rice, preserved meat and fish. They were often presented in huge baskets and I'd always see plenty of shoppers grabbing small handfuls of tiny dried fish and slyly popping them into their mouths like I would with grapes or cherries from supermarkets in Australia. There was a whole tofu section. I wanted to but always baulked at trying Shanghai's famous smelly tofu. In the preparation stage I thought it smelled like rotting garbage doused in stale urine. The tofu is fermented in a brine and then fried, which knocks off a bit of the stink. But I didn't think something smelling that bad belonged in my mouth, even though I'd been told it was a 'must try'. There were plenty of other forms of tofu including the soft variety and smoked or fried tofu that was good in stir-frys. I didn't know my way around bean curd well enough to ever buy any, but *ayi* Tina generally included a tofu dish in the weekly meal she made for us.

I bought most of our vegetables at the market. I became addicted to being able to buy cheap tomatoes that tasted like real tomatoes, rather than those hard, insipid looking tomatoes that had been plucked unripe from the vine and stored for weeks before being presented at some supermarket fruit and veg sections. It was all about the produce being fresh. And that also meant seasonal. It was actually a pleasure not to be able to buy fruit and vegetables year round that had been put in cold storage and imported from around the world, but having to roll with what had just been plucked off the farm.

In Shanghai it was important to know the specific foods for specific seasons as well as the foods for special occasions. We were amazed at all the different celebrations, occasions and holidays in China – and that there was a dumpling for every occasion. Smarty was more adventurous than me when it came to tasting all the different dumplings and specialities for the events. I baulked after I embarrassingly started retching from a salted duck egg and lotus paste mooncake I tried during the Mid-Autumn Festival.

Different festivals feature different dumplings in different parts of the country, but they are all said to represent family reunion and harmony. The flour for the dumplings is usually made out of wheat or rice, but there are countless stuffings and ways of rolling, cutting, shaping and cooking the dough. It was said that Zhuge Liang, considered one of China's greatest strategists, made the first dumpling about 1800 years ago. He made human-head-sized dumplings as sacrifices to comfort the spirits of soldiers who were facing being slain in battle. The big dough balls were symbols of the soldiers' heads and were dropped into a river before battle to ask the gods for victory.

Jiaozi are the crescent-shaped dumplings eaten at Chinese New Year, or Spring Festival. Families all get together to make *jiaozi* and sometimes hide a coin or a sweet in a dumpling. Whoever gets the coin is believed to have good luck for the year – much the same as the English tradition of adding a silver penny to a plum pud.

Tangyuan are the celebrated dumpling eaten during the Lantern Festival, which signals the end of Chinese New Year celebrations. The traditional sticky rice dumplings are made with sweet fillings, like sweetened sesame or peanuts. The more exotic *tangyuan* are very pretty and colourful because they have strawberry juice, mango juice or green tea powder mixed in with the glutinous flour.

The Qingming Festival in early April is also called the Tomb-Sweeping Festival. It is a time for Chinese people to pay their respects to their ancestors and visit and clean the graves of relatives. They may also offer sacrifices to their ancestors, burn paper money and fly kites – during the day and at night with glowing coloured lanterns on the kite strings. They eat *qingtuan*, a green round-shaped dumpling stuffed with sweet bean paste. The green colour comes from the green plum juice in which the dumpling has been soaked.

The Dragon Boat Festival falls on the fifth day of the fifth month of the Chinese calendar. *Zongzi* are eaten during the Dragon Boat Festival to commemorate the death of Qu Yuan, a poet who ended his life by jumping into a river. The story goes that people tossed *zongzi* into the river so that fish would eat the dumplings and spare the man. *Zongzi* are made of glutinous or sticky rice stuffed with fillings and wrapped in bamboo leaves to make a pyramid-shape, then steamed or boiled. Stuffings can be sweet or savoury. Our friend Jane offered us a taste of *zongzi* made by her mother. It was an enormous dumpling stuffed with meat and was like a complete meal. Smarty really enjoyed it and, apart from letting me have a small taste, chewed his way through the whole lot. Afterwards he said he felt like he'd eaten a brick.

Mooncakes are a fundamental element of the Mid-Autumn Festival of late September. The festival is all about remembering or reuniting with family and loved ones at a time when it is said everyone, living and deceased, would share the same full moon. Mooncakes are shared during the festival. They are usually round and quite thick. While the pastry is thin, the filling is very dense. The traditional mooncake is filled with lotus paste, with a salty duck egg in the middle representing the moon, but there are also variations containing jujube paste or red bean paste. I'd been told the red bean paste mooncake tasted a little like a Cherry Ripe. The comparison was way off.

After urging the children to always try something before declaring they didn't like it, I felt we needed to follow our own advice – even when we weren't always sure of what we were about to put in our mouths in Shanghai. I would never have known mooncakes were not for me had I not tried one. And of course it's polite to at least try a nibble of what you have been offered. It was how Sam, our colleague at the *Shanghai Daily*, found out he didn't really like a special Chinese candy made from bird saliva. Smarty arrived at work one day to find the Chinese feature writers abuzz over a treat one had been given and had brought into the office to share. He saw the treat, that looked like an off-white thick and hairy corded fairy-floss, just as Sam tore off a chunk and popped it in his mouth. The look on Sam's face as he tried to gulp down the candy made from the spit of a swallow caused so much amusement for the entire features department, Smarty thought it was more polite that he didn't have a taste of the delicacy lest he produce an even worse reaction.

Having shunned some of Shanghai's special occasion delicacies, we did try most dishes that were delivered to us in restaurants. We had been presented with duck tongue in chilli sauce, red pepper pig's ear, sweet geese liver and hot pot bullfrogs – all without really meaning to be. At a weekend lunch one day with Chinese friends Peter and Michelle we confessed to our utter incompetence at ordering. Peter told us not to worry as he would order for us all and was going to give us a taste of many special Shanghai dishes. Michelle asked if there was anything we wouldn't eat and we boldly told her we were willing to put our tastebuds in their hands – as long as they didn't tell us anything that they thought might scare us too much until after we'd eaten it. Peter might have only been teasing, but I think we might have eaten snake.

I decided it was much safer sampling tea. Tea is much more than a tradition in China. It is like a faith and its devotees are happy to discuss its qualities for hours. It can be quite entrancing. I quickly became immune to feeling embarrassed at admitting my ignorance over matters so intrinsic to the Chinese culture as tea, the ancient art of tea making, and even the significance of all the different styles of clay and porcelain teapots to be found. I told my Australian friend

Bianca, who'd developed quite a strong local knowledge, that I wanted to understand tea, I just didn't know how or where to start. Bianca decided to take me to a tea market, *cha chen*, called Tianshan Tea Mall at 520 Zhongshan Xie Lu near her place in Changning district. The mall was like a massive warehouse with tea sellers in booths and nooks and lovely little shops on one floor and stall after stall overflowing with the most beautiful tea sets on the other. There was so much tea. There was so much to learn about tea. I just hoped the essence of a fine tea was similar to that of a fine wine: if you like it, then it's a good drop.

In China, tea is generally categorised as green tea, black tea, dark tea (which is typically Pu'er tea), oolong tea, white tea and flower tea. For a tea novice, it's important to know that there's a recommended vessel for every type of tea. Flower tea should be served in a glass cup, green tea in a glass or china cup, oolong tea in a red porcelain teapot and black tea in a coffee pot and cup. With Bianca and our friend Alegre from New York, I sat down to be served tea in a corner of a teapot shop. There were four Chinese women already drinking tea and the tea house woman busied herself making a pot and setting out little tea cups before us. There were all sorts of tea leaves around us and the combined smell of the leaves and the tea being prepared was rich and sweet and lovely. I watched enthralled as the tea maker shared in conversation with the Chinese women while her fine-fingered hands moved deftly, measuring the tea, opening and then closing the lid on the teapot and gracefully pouring the tea. I felt so clumsy and awkward, as I often did around Chinese women, and actually talked myself out of buying one of the complete tea sets and lovely carved wooden serving trays. I knew I'd manage to drop it or spill tea everywhere every time I brought out the set and my whole tea making experience would end up with me feeling like an oaf. I was so captivated by the pleasantness of the scene before me I managed to miss my mouth with my dainty teacup and spilled my tea all down my jacket. Luckily I didn't have to go and clean myself up or I'd have missed one of those conversations that could only happen in China.

One of the Chinese women enjoying the tea was pregnant. So was Alegre. So was Bianca. The pregnant Chinese woman spoke a little English. She confided she was having a boy. She was delighted. We were amazed. How could she know? China's one-child policy was introduced in 1979. In Shanghai and across China during this time the number of boys born has been significantly more than the number of girls. The gender imbalance is said to be the result of years of sex-selective abortion of girls. As a result, doctors and ultrasound technicians have been banned from revealing the sex of the baby to any expectant parent. Alegre, who was planning to have her baby in a Chinese hospital, could not find out the sex of her unborn baby. The fact she was a foreigner and the baby was her second child did not loosen the restrictions on the sex being revealed. The Chinese woman laughed and said she was sure she was having a boy. She said nobody had been bribed and nobody had broken a law. But she said the Chinese always found a way of getting around the tight controls. I thought she was probably a member of the first generation of Chinese born after the implementation of the one-child policy. They are all now approaching their 30s and having a considerable impact on Chinese society. It is a generation that is better educated, wealthier, more worldly and open-minded than any previous generation. It is a generation that is also more accustomed to getting what they want. 'It's really very easy,' she said. 'If the doctor ever tells you congratulations, you know you're having a boy.'

CHAPTER 21

WHO COULD BE CRANKY AT CINDERELLA?

As modern and as Western as Shanghai and the Shanghainese sometimes appeared, it could be an illusion. Underneath the shiny commercial surface of the city and behind the designer sunglasses, business suits and materialistic get-ahead bravado of its citizens, Shanghai and its people hold dear to tradition. Shanghai is unmistakably China. There are very Chinese habits.

Milly and Nelson embraced the Chinese as they saw them and even picked up some of the Chinese traits. It was great watching the kids trying to use their chopsticks and I felt so proud watching them playing a game where they were both picking up dried beans with chopsticks and counting them out in Mandarin as they placed the beans back into a bowl. Within just a few months of our arrival, Nelson began making the two-fingered peace sign that so many Chinese did whenever anyone took his photograph. The kids were accustomed to washing their hands every five minutes as everything that could be touched in China had the capacity to cause illness. They were also happy not only to wear shoes outside, but put on their 'inside shoes' at home or in the classroom as no-one ever went barefoot in China. It was a long way from the struggle we had getting them to wear clothes when we first arrived. They even got cranky at me in the mornings if I appeared without wearing slippers. Milly wholeheartedly adopted one other Chinese habit. As we walked along the street, I found her stopping to spit on footpaths, on garden beds, on trees and on patches of grass. She said she wanted inside her body to be 'harmonious' so everything yukky had to come out. I assumed they taught her that at school. Nelson was even worse. I caught my little two-year-old sitting down watching television with two fingers up to his mouth and his lips puckered. When I asked him what he was doing, he nonchalantly replied: 'Cigaretting'.

There are more than 350 million smokers in China. Shanghai was the first city in the nation to encourage hospitals to set up clinics to help people to quit smoking. Making things difficult was that about 40 per cent of hospital doctors smoked. China is the world's biggest cigarette producer. Cigarettes in China are cheap and are not taxed. Some of my smoking colleagues said they also just enjoyed buying the ubiquitous Chinese cigarette brands such as 'Happiness', or 'Double Happiness' – they said no-one ever died from happiness. About 66 per cent of men in Shanghai smoked, compared to about

3 per cent of women. Smoking was widely permitted – 35 per cent of workplaces allowed smoking. Smoking was common in restaurants and grocery stores. It was only banned in hospitals and schools in 1997 in an update to the Shanghai Regulation of Smoking Restriction in Public Areas. I thought it was quite amusing that my son followed most of his activities by having a rest and 'cigaretting', but my friends in Australia were horrified. I took it as his way of relating to being a man in China and that he would have totally kicked the habit by the time he was four.

While it was terrific to observe, I found it hard to get to know very many Chinese people. The language barrier made it hard to connect with many Chinese who hadn't been raised or at least spent some time abroad, but so too did some of the intrinsic differences between the cultures and the ignorance of foreigners like me as to acceptable ways of communicating. I knew that 'face', or *mianzi* in Chinese, was a big deal in China. I also knew I had insufficient understanding of face to avoid making mistakes when dealing with sensitive subjects. The most basic principle of face seems to be always remaining respectful and polite. But there's much more than being well-mannered, so when it came to discussions in which I thought the Chinese may take even the slightest offence or feel criticised, I adopted a policy of erring on the side of staying silent.

I felt it was a shame. It seemed to me that many Chinese were caught up in a contradiction and I would have enjoyed being able to get local perspective on my observation. They seemed to be living a manically frenzied and productive life to earn enough money to live and afford all the education and enrichment classes to give their child every opportunity for advancement, but were also trying to cling to many of the traditional traits of living a balanced life which encouraged calm and retaining a harmonious connection with the environment. So many Chinese just seemed so busy and had to constantly push so they or their children could get ahead, that it had bred a competitive fear that had become part of their make-up. It seemed they believed that if they stopped pushing even for a moment, they would get left behind. It seemed to be isolating them from their fellow Chinese to the point everyone was seen as a rival rather than a neighbour. And while many Chinese who I saw were quick to offer a smile, they didn't seem to have time to be happy. I felt very comfortable discussing most things with my Chinese friends, but ultimately felt I shouldn't raise this topic lest it cause offence.

Face plays a major part in almost all interactions and is a very important element of the Chinese culture. While I enjoyed a good argument and revelled in lively dinner debates, I was told such behaviour could make Chinese people uncomfortable. I think the mutual and playful mocking of each other that Smarty and I invariably indulged in when we were out as a couple would also not sit well. Public displays of anger or emotion were to be avoided under the general rules of maintaining face. And negative answers to requests should never come as a direct 'no'.

Both Smarty and I found communicating with the staff at work like walking on eggshells, especially as part of our job each day was to rework stories filed by the reporters and explain to them the problems. It was very difficult to avoid sounding critical when a deadline was approaching and there were so many stories that didn't make sense or had so many basic facts missing they should not even have been in the newspaper. We both tried, although I felt concentrating on all the positives and softly touching on the negatives was a little like dealing with a recalcitrant toddler rather than a grown up professional journalist. The frustration was compounded as our professional pride, as well as management's judgement of our performance, was based on the quality of the stories that actually appeared in the paper, without regard to the mess we were often first presented with and the efforts we had made to respectfully coax a better story out of the reporters.

Ultimately, I fear my efforts at appropriate communication in the workplace faltered. I think I managed to do some serious face damage when I asked my editor at the *Shanghai Daily* for the reason she denied my request to change shifts. I'd seen my editor loudly berate people on a daily basis in a manner that seemed at odds with what I know of the concept of face. Her behaviour seemed primarily aimed at humiliating her subordinates publicly. She often behaved in a way I would consider inappropriate in any workplace by loudly calling people 'stupid', rather than confining her comments to the issue that caused the problem. Thinking she was the kind of woman who favoured a direct, no-nonsense form of communication, I decided to approach her about my shift change request while she was seated in the newsroom with her deputy in charge of staff management. To my mind we had a polite and direct discussion between adults over an issue that was important in maintaining a good working relationship. I felt I managed to make it clear why I wanted to switch shifts, she explained why she thought it was not possible, and we tried to clear up any misunderstandings. Unfortunately I found out later, this was not the way the discussion was seen by the Chinese. I'm still not sure which rules I broke, but I was told there were many. I'm also still unsure whether I had face, lost it or caused the loss of it. My reputation had apparently been shot. I was advised to stick to the more acceptable route of whinging behind management's back.

Differences in communication methods are not only confined to the workplace in China and aren't always about Westerners offending Chinese sensibilities. There are topics that are freely discussed in China that aren't regarded as polite in the West. Such as money. It was common to be asked how much you earned and how much you paid, for everything. Of course, foreigners were always told we'd paid too much. We usually did. Not only did foreigners pay more than Chinese for the same items, Western-style products and services came at very inflated prices. There were generally three opening prices when buying something in China: one for tourists, one for expats who lived locally and spoke some Chinese, then there was the Chinese price. Chinese women who had married foreign men told me they rarely let their husbands go shopping or even tag along when they were trying to buy something. The very presence of the non-Chinese partner often caused the price tag to skyrocket.

I'm not sure I ever got the Chinese price, except perhaps once when I went to have my hair trimmed at a local hairdresser. Smarty kept showing up at home with shorter and shorter hair. Eventually he told me he was becoming addicted to getting haircuts. At the hairdresser he would have his hair washed, get a 20 minute head massage, then a shoulder massage, then an arm and hand massage, and at the end of it all, a quick haircut. It all cost him about 20 yuan (A$3.26). I decided it was time I had a go. I put the children down for an afternoon nap, waited for *ayi* Tina to arrive and then dashed to the closest hairdresser with a note from Tina asking for a trim. While I sat in the chair, one assistant lathered my head with a lovely-smelling shampoo and massaged for about 15 minutes. I was then taken to have my hair rinsed, where I scored another head massage, and then escorted back to my seat where my hair was piled up high on my head and I was given a relaxing shoulder and arm massage. Finally after all this massaging and rubbing, the official hairdresser closed in on me, whipped the towel covering my hair from my head and almost screamed. My hair was in the most incredible tangle. He couldn't get a comb through it. Assistants applied conditioners and brought out wide-toothed combs and brushes and worked on me from both sides, pulling and teasing, but still the knots stuck. I eventually had to take matters into my own hands and detangle my hair myself. At the end of it all I was furious. My hair was a mess and my scalp hurt from all the yanking and knot pulling. But I was charged only 5 yuan (A$0.80).

In Shanghai, foreigners are often struck by how cheap things are but can be clueless as to how much things should really cost. It is part of the adjustment process to accept that bargaining is part of almost every transaction. It initially felt awkward bargaining, but I eventually found a rhythm and learned to very much enjoy the process, especially at markets. However, I never got over my feelings of awkwardness arguing over money or discussing earnings. Yet most Chinese people we encountered didn't suffer from these feelings. When I was involved in the traffic accident with the taxi and the motorbike rider, the crowd did not seem in any way concerned about banding together to come up with an amount I needed to pay as compensation and demanding I fork this arbitrary sum over. When we rented our apartment, we found there were payment requests we didn't expect. Yet they were so boldly demanded, and we felt so uncomfortable arguing over the money, we paid up. My friend Jane one night told us a story that we thought exemplified the Chinese practical perspective on money and candour in discussing the topic. She was telling us how she and her Swedish husband met and began dating. 'Every night he'd take me out to dinner,' she said. 'Every night we'd go to a different restaurant in Xintiandi,' (a restored pedestrian strip full of upmarket restaurants, shops and boutiques). 'If I knew he would be my husband, I would never have let him take me there. I would never have let him spend the money.'

The Chinese are ever practical. There isn't a lot of room for romanticism regarding day to day life even in a relatively affluent city like Shanghai. Work, earning money, finding a husband or wife, having a child and giving that child every chance to get ahead would appear to take precedence over recreation and dreams. There does, however, seem one outlet of whimsy amongst the Chinese. It is the choice of their English name. I met a man named Skye, a female Summer, a female Cloudy, and a male Shy. I've also come across a Rainbow and a Bobbo, but my favourite was Cinderella. It might all sound very funny at first, but I soon began to think it might be Chinese shrewdness at work. As our friend Federico observed, trying to complain to a company manager over a document he wanted couriered across the city, only for it to be lost, then recovered, then delivered to the wrong address: 'How can you get really cross with a girl named Cinderella?'

CHAPTER 22

BLUE ANTS TO BEDTIME

I'd broken rules of face and Propaganda Department orders, so it should have come as no surprise to learn I'd also inadvertently made other workplace errors. Apparently, my fashion sense in Shanghai was also upside-down. It seemed that it was okay for women of any age to wear skirts that barely covered their bottoms. But it was a rarity and, I sensed, frowned upon in the *Shanghai Daily* office, to wear a shirt revealing flesh below the collar bone. Wearing an everyday deep-V or a wide-neck shirt, I felt utterly exposed compared to my female Chinese colleagues. That was until I saw the amount of Chinese leg on display. I put it down to just another difference between us.

It was hard to get a grip on Shanghai style as it ranged from designer to the everyday and the extraordinary. There was also downright daft with women, men and children getting about in T-shirts and jackets emblazoned with crazily out-of-place English phrases like 'Up Yours', 'Minnie Mouse is widely known as Mickey's friend', 'Not Nothing', 'Thing's Hot', 'How There?' and on babies, 'Cute baby smells'.

On Nanjing Lu, high fashions were flaunted and business attire looked chic and sharp. Top designers had street-level stores with the latest fashions in beautifully dressed windows. The stores sat alongside jewellers and watchmakers and perfume outlets and shoe boutiques. It was an opulent display of luxury and deluxe-end brands under giant spot-lit posters of Claudia Schiffer in Salvatore Ferragamo, Linda Evangelista in Prada and Agyness Deyne in Burberry. The big-name international fashion chain stores were also omnipresent in Shanghai. H&M, Zara, Esprit, Bossini and kidswear brand Les Enphants all had a number of outlets, as did China's own Me and City.

In Shanghai anything could be copied. Young Chinese women paraded in versions of the latest trends. It was difficult to tell which were real and which were fakes. There were so many tailors, knock-offs, cheap brand name handbags and sunglasses that everyone on the high streets appeared reasonably well attired. Even some of the women who trotted around in over-the-top taffeta and silk cocktail dresses seemed to sort of make it work as office wear. Some, not all. Chinese domestic workers also generally dressed smartly. Even a woman I saw regularly who spent her days collecting recycling, discarded bicycle wheels and old furniture on Huashan Lu wore fitted jackets and heels on the street.

The emphasis on clothing and fashion in Shanghai is a far cry from 30 years ago when rationing coupons were needed for almost all daily necessities. The now booming textile industry was lagging. Clothing colour options were restricted to blue, grey and brown. A retired senior Communist Party official, Chen Jinhua, said a comment by French journalist Robert Guillain, in which he jokingly referred to the Chinese drab-dressers as 'blue ants under the red flag' troubled Party leaders so much that it contributed to China's decision in the 1970s to engage with developed Western countries to bolster the economy.

Chen's anecdote in a memoir called *The Eventful Years* was released just as I was deciding whether or not to invest in some new jackets for the upcoming Shanghai winter. It was an important decision I was making. If I did purchase the new jacket, it would be a signal we might stay in Shanghai to endure a second winter. It would mean we were considering staying another whole year – I couldn't imagine needing big overcoats or a down knee-length jacket on the Gold Coast. Our clothes really could affect our lives. Chen said clothes affected the lives of millions. He said in September 1971, Chairman Mao Zedong toured Changsha, the capital of Hunan Province. He gave staff the day off to look around. Chen said when one female worker returned to base she was very excited. 'When Mao asked what had come over her, she replied: "I bought a pair of terylene trousers after standing in a queue for ages."' The terylene pants did not wrinkle like cotton pants and had a smart, straight crease. Chen said Mao told his advisors to go and buy the technology. It was the beginning of a massive round of importing technology and equipment for textile and farming industries to China from the West.

China is now the world's largest textile and clothing producer. Nearly all branch offices, buying offices and production bases of foreign clothing and fashion brands in China are located in Shanghai. Shanghai also produces about 10 per cent of foreign-brand leather goods and 17 per cent of foreign brand ladies shoes. Some elements of Shanghai's very own fashion palette, however, have not changed with this growth.

Shanghai had me thinking of making a Chinese version of a ridiculous but very funny short film I once saw. The basic premise, and possibly the name of the piece, was: How far From the Beach is it Acceptable to Wear Your Underwear? It started with a guy wearing white Y-fronts on Sydney's Bondi Beach, where few beach-goers looked askance. He progressed to the Campbell Parade esplanade of the celeb-filled, iconic beachside suburb where he still only attracted a few querying looks as he strutted about in nothing but undies (although he may also have worn thongs, the footwear, as well. We do have some dress standards in Australia.) He carried on testing the theory of people's acceptance of inappropriate dress and underpant-tolerance on buses, in the city-centre shopping mall, sightseeing towers, office blocks, the city's outer suburbs, county towns, and ultimately as far from the beach as possible – in the outback.

In Shanghai, I thought it was also a theory worth testing – on pyjamas. How far from the Shanghainese bedroom was it socially acceptable to wear nightclothes? I originally thought it was the proximity of our home to numerous hospitals that lay behind the great number of pyjama-wearers I encountered. Then it wasn't so close to the hospital that I began noticing the phenomenon, or in the middle of the night, or even early morning.

I saw one woman cycling around the bazaars near Yuyuan Gardens wearing pyjamas and high heels. They were nice pyjamas. It was also about 11 a.m. And the number of times I saw men out for a stroll, a smoke and a chat in their pyjamas and dress shoes just blocks from Nanjing Xie Lu was ridiculous. Smarty and I tried to outdo each other with odd pyjama-wearer sightings. A seemingly dapper middle-aged gent squiring a fashionable young woman emerged from a Fuxing Lu clothing store around midday – she in a frock and heels, he in pyjamas and brogues. Another popped out of a Xikang Lu hairdressers about 4.30 p.m. dressed for bed. On the Bund, a man was taking in the view wearing pyjamas, loafers and a cravat. On the corner of Weihei Lu and Shaanxi Bei Lu, a man performed the magnificent feat of riding his bicycle to transport a regulation-sized refrigerator, in peak hour traffic, wearing his pyjamas.

Carl Crow, in his book *Foreign Devils in the Flowery Kingdom*, wrote of the Chinese bewilderment at Western Griffins (these days called 'newbies') getting around in our fitted and comparatively uncomfortable attire. Crow, an American author and newspaperman who helped create the modern advertising industry in China, lived in Shanghai for 25 years in the early 1900s. He noted then, and it's perhaps still relevant now, that the traditional Chinese are the ones who have the right dress sense and our puzzling at their pyjama-as-clothes style is more than matched by their amusement at what we and the younger generation of Chinese are wearing.

I have to admit I was amused at the number of Western women who thought they might look great in a *qipao*. It's almost a must-have souvenir from China and each time I visited the South Bund Soft-Spinning Material Market at Lujiabang Lu I saw countless foreign women being measured and fitted for the custom-made Chinese dress. The *qipao* is as symbolic of China as the kimono is of Japan. It was the height of fashion in Shanghai in the 1930s when the city was flush with cash and jazz music and the race track, elegant women and political intrigue were all part of the lure of the port city's prime areas under the control of the Americans, British and French.

It added to the peculiarity of the whole experience that so many women chose to wear *qipao* to the Australian Women's Social Group Melbourne Cup Lunch I decided to attend in Shanghai. It was the first, and only, overtly Australian function in China I agreed to go to. I'm not a huge horse racing fan, but am acutely aware of the exalted place of the Cup in the Australian culture, have attended a number of Melbourne Cups at Flemington and have often surprised myself by feeling far more curious about the horses and their form on Cup day than fashions in the field. And never, not as far back as I can cast my memory, have I missed dropping whatever was at hand — school spelling tests/work interviews/babies at the breast (not dropping them literally) — to scramble to the nearest television to watch the horses career 3200 metres around the track on the first Tuesday in November.

But I felt vaguely uncomfortable at the Melbourne Cup in Shanghai. We'd made such an effort not to live the separatist expat lifestyle and to learn and experience what we could of China, that it didn't seem right to all of a sudden coagulate into a such foreign group and just be so ... Australian.

But it was the Melbourne Cup. I wasn't one of the many women wearing a *qipao*, but wished I was. It would have completed the ridiculousness of the picture as I joined the champagne drinking, bellowed at a giant screen displaying the race and tossed tickets in the air as we cursed horses who failed to live up to their promise and breeding, even though we had never heard of any of them until we picked them up in the sweep. We rued not being able to bet – the ban on gambling imposed in 1949 meant betting on horse races was illegal in China. The Australian accents grew stronger and the conversation veered dangerously into Okker cliché. But we didn't care. The strains of trying to act according to the codes and mores of another culture were able to be tossed momentarily aside. We were back again among friends who knew thongs were fashionable footwear, who knew cockies were birds and birds were women, who knew a pie wasn't a chart, but full of meat and gravy. The only thing funnier than the boisterous arguments and hearty cackles from a roomful of Aussies was the amused bewilderment on the faces of some of the other foreign women attending their first ever Melbourne Cup. And the fact that in our Cup goodies bag there was a voucher for a discount on Botox treatments. I actually called up about the Botox offer. The beautician asked me if I was interested in the Chinese or the American version. When I asked the difference she deadpanned that the Chinese version was cheaper, unlikely to work as well and would have to be replaced far quicker than the overseas product. Of course it was.

After the function was done, things became even more absurd. We gathered for an after party at Sasha's on Dong Ping Lu in the French Concession. It should have been an utterly incongruous scene – a group of Australians and other foreigners drinking and laying claim for the evening to the garden of one of Shanghai's historic houses, the 1920s French manor house formerly owned by Charlie Soong. Soong boasted immense wealth and influence, but was even more famous as the father of the three Soong sisters who played such a vital role in shaping modern China. The youngest, Mei Ling, married the leader of Nationalist China and later of Taiwan, Chiang Kai-shek. The middle daughter, Soong Ching Ling, became known as 'Mother of the Nation'. She married founder of the Chinese Republic, Dr Sun Yat-sen, and after his death was appointed one of the three non-communist vice chairs of the People's Republic of China and served as acting head of state of communist China from 1976 to 1978. The eldest sister, Ai Ling, was originally Sun Yat-sen's secretary but went on to marry H. H. Kung, finance minister of the Nationalist government.

In the beer garden at the back of the Soong's Shanghai house was where I snapped back into reality at the end of a very long Melbourne Cup Day. I was all dressed up and ready to keep celebrating all things Australian. But I wasn't at home. I was in China. And I felt very conspicuously and suddenly very awkwardly like a foreigner in Shanghai.

CHAPTER 23

FEAR AND TIMING IN SHANGHAI

Despite China being the only country in the world whose ancient civilisation has been passed down continuously for more than 5000 years, the melting pot nature of Shanghai has made the city quite open to finding a space for foreign cultural events as well as Chinese traditions. Being part of Shanghai's expat community, we celebrated not only the Melbourne Cup and AFL Grand Final Day, but also Easter, Valentine's Day, Thanksgiving, a Swedish Christmas and Halloween.

While we tried to experience as much as we could of China, we ultimately decided to jump aboard these occasions, especially those which had also been embraced by many Chinese. Valentine's Day in

Shanghai is a huge event and treated with the same sort of significance it attracts in the United States – which is generally far more uninhibited than the demonstrations of love by Australia's romantics. In Shanghai on Valentine's Day, restaurants are booked out, roses are bought and delivered by the millions and thousands of couples get married. About 800 couples get married each day in Shanghai, but the number jumps three-fold on Valentine's Day.

This acceptance and willingness by not only the expats but also the Chinese to revel in Western festivals was how I came to be an Australian mum roped into helping organise trick or treat for Halloween in China. I was uncertain as to what one actually did with a Halloween pumpkin. I knew of no traditional Halloween activities beyond trick or treat. And I had no clue whether costumes were meant to be scary or just a chance for the kids to have a bit of fun and dress up. I had agreed to host a post-trick-or-treat Halloween party for the children of One Park Avenue and was feeling a little out of my depth. My American friend Lindsay tried to calm me by telling me it was fine for the kids to dress up as fairies, princesses or Batman as they didn't really have to be scary. She told me her two daughters were dressing up as brides. As soon as the words came out of her mouth we both realised there might not be many things scarier than seeing our daughters dressed up to marry, especially when they were under five.

After locking in a safe route through the One Park Avenue towers for groups of costumed expat and Chinese children, schooling the majority of children on how to get involved in this 'foreign tradition', greeting parents and learning how to trick or treat in about eight different languages, running after the children to smear their hands with antibacterial wipes before they shoved each handful of treats into their mouths, and checking all of the treats to make sure they didn't contain contaminated milk or egg products, the trick or treat seemed a success. At my after party, where I had tried to evoke the Halloween spirit by hanging up as many cut-out paper pumpkins and plastic spiders, bats and skeletons as possible, I resorted to my usual repertoire of party entertainment. I fear, however, a treasure hunt, duck-duck-goose and musical statues failed as traditional Halloween activities. The children seemed to enjoy it, but I'm not sure I would ever be called on to host a party for such an American tradition in China again.

The Chinese willingness to embrace elements of Western culture is often seen in Shanghai as an important part of being progressive and fashionable. One of the most obvious manifestations of this trend is the way the Shanghainese speak. Pidgin English is fashionable. In Shanghai, it's called Yangjingbang English. It's a snappy mixture of English and Chinese with influences from Canton, Indian and Portugese that combines to create a kind of short-hand communication. The *Shanghai Daily* explained that Yangjingbang English emerged from the Yangjingbang area of old Shanghai very close to the Bund that has since been transformed into Yan'an Road East. Yangjingbang was a small tributary of the Huangpu River that became the boundary between the British and French concessions in 1848. It was where cargo ships docked from India, Japan, Europe and the US. Ferries from the suburbs anchored there and Chinese middlemen hustled along the riverbanks to help make business possible between Westerners who spoke no Chinese and the Chinese, for a fee. Yangjingbang English became the language of commerce in old Shanghai. While the Yangjingbang waterway itself has disappeared – it was filled in and paved over by the French and British because it got too polluted – many of the terms have remained in use in Shanghai, especially among white collars. *Ha pi* in Shanghai dialect sounds like and translates as happy. Other commonly used words include *fan si* (face), *pai si* (pass), *bas hi* (bus) and *shui men ting* (cement).

The Shanghainese have long been open to adapting and exploiting economic opportunities with foreigners. It was one of the reasons Shanghai was expected to be one of cities most adept at rising out of the global financial crisis. Far from the global financial crisis being seen as a disaster, the downturn from its first incarnation was considered an opportunity for Shanghai to overtake other cities battered by the crisis, such as New York and London, and turn itself into an international financial and shipping hub.

Shanghai's economy cooled when the severity of the financial crisis became screamingly apparent around the world in September due predominantly to Shanghai's large exposure to foreign markets, compared with other Chinese mainland cities. Shanghai's economic growth for the year eased overall to 9.7 per cent – high by worldwide standards, but the city's first single-digit performance since 1992. The city's service industry, including financial firms, catering and property companies, grew 11.3 per cent to 735 billion yuan. This growth rate however was significantly down from a 15.2 per cent gain the year before. The industrial sector experienced diminishing growth of 8.2 per cent, compared with 11.5 per cent the year before. The output value of high-quality steel manufacturing fell 7.9 per cent and the auto industry experienced an 0.9 per cent drop. The city's exports increased 17.7 per cent, down from 26.7 per cent in 2007. Areas of weakening export included communications equipment, computers, clothing and textiles, furniture and pharmaceuticals.

On the street, the first wave of the crisis caused a similarly unsettling ripple. The feeling was that China remained in a strong position coming off a smoking growth rate of 13 per cent in 2007 and that the government was reacting quickly to stimulate the economy and immunise the country from the global downturn. The city's small and medium enterprises were bracing for losses in incomes and slackening demand, especially export-oriented companies, but domestically people still seemed willing to spend, particularly as incomes continued to rise. It meant despite the portent of financial misery, Shanghai's rich remained rich. The trappings of wealth were still flaunted in Shanghai. But the poor were feeling the pinch. Many *ayi* were thrown out of jobs as wealthy Chinese and expat families started shedding some of their domestic luxuries in preparation for leaner times. Factory workers too were laid off as declining consumption in America and overseas markets forced factory cutbacks and closures. With many migrant workers suddenly out of work in Shanghai I did notice an increase in the visible poor. More migrants suddenly seemed to be on the streets selling lotus root and berries or shining shoes. The number of women and children out begging at night on Nanjing Lu, positioning themselves under billboards of a gold-bathed Charlize Theron for J'adore and bejewelled Eva Green for Montblanc, seemed to jump. And they weren't as easy to shake. It may sound condescending and I may have overestimated my ability to help, but I did hope the few yuan I regularly handed over to one particular mum and her small child made a difference.

Even though we were in Shanghai as employees and not as business managers or operators, Smarty and I did feel the less optimisic pall that began to pervade Shanghai's frenetic development. We thought perhaps it was prudent to consider our future in Shanghai and our commitment to living in China. We'd taken the children down to pick out a Disney movie as a treat from our favourite DVD shops – 'World Movies' and another store called 'Even Better Than World Movies' immediately opposite it on Dagu Lu – then on to lunch. It was at lunch with our friend Alegre, while watching the kids creating a scene with the locals by throwing scraps of Indian dhosa to an ever-increasing flock of sparrows, that we started counting our friends who were experiencing the effects of the downturn. While few were in as dire a situation as Alegre and her husband Dan, an architect who was looking for a new job after the project he was working on stalled, most had been affected to a degree. Many expats were having their financial packages cut back, others were returning home to their head office or remaining behind while their family relocated back to their home country. Others were reassessing their business plans and looking for options that included tailoring their products to the Chinese market rather than exporting.

While we were talking I received a text message from the agency that Milly occasionally did some modelling work for. Milly had gone along with some friends in early summer to a photo shoot with a Shanghai photographer called Victor Cheng. She seemed to very much enjoy the process of dressing up and playing naturally in front of the camera for clients such as Les Enphants and Disney Baby. She got to wear lovely clothes and be fawned over by fashion and hair stylists, do her best to follow some of the mimed gestures and poses demonstrated by the photographer's assistants, and hang out with a few other Chinese and expat children who were also attending the shoots. She was paid – about as much for a couple of hours work as I was for an entire day – and treated to a lunch that invariably consisted of chicken nuggets and chips. She also often got special treats to take home, including goldfish and turtles. I drew the line when she said she was allowed to bring home a rabbit.

The studio were calling because they urgently wanted her to be in a shoot for a clothing catalogue. She wasn't keen and we felt quite esconced in the restaurant. 'Sorry, timing doesn't work for us,' I sent in a return SMS. I didn't expect the reply: 'Who is timing?' Amid the chuckles at the misunderstanding, I thought it just went to show that even in the simplest of exchanges there was always room in China for misinterpretations and differences. And I thought that maybe we really should be thinking a whole lot more seriously about our timing and future in China.

CHAPTER 24

IT FEELS LIKE HOME

'Do you think you might be ready to go home?' Smarty seemed as though he had something important to say and wasn't going to be subtle in broaching the idea of leaving China.

He was ready. A new arm of a media company was in the process of being established in Australia operating a centralised sub-editing and design hub for papers around the nation. Smarty had been sounded out about the role as chief sub-editor. After a few days of mulling over the implications, he said he couldn't deny he felt a real professional excitement about the job and was keen to relocate back to Australia. The job was in Brisbane. We could move back to our home at the Gold Coast. His mind seemed already there.

I agreed that we both needed a break from the *Shanghai Daily*. The experience had been enlightening and valuable in learning about China and the way the country's media operated. While we felt frustrated that we hadn't been able to impart a great deal of knowledge or assistance to the Chinese staff, we had certainly been given a lesson. We'd learned much about working in a foreign environment and developing workplace diplomacy. But we were convinced we could gain little more in terms of professional development by staying. If anything, we felt remaining at the paper longer might begin to blunt our news sense and fuzzy our ability to filter out rhetoric to get to the facts. In order to fit in and mentally endure some of the requirements of the job, we'd suppressed so many of the instincts that we had developed in our careers. As a result, we were worried we were losing our edge. And we did want to work back in the Western media after our China encounter.

But did leaving the *Shanghai Daily* mean we really had to leave Shanghai? There were still work opportunities galore in the city. Despite the slowdown in growth many top end businesses, including Australian companies, were still developing. Shanghai was also preparing to host the 2010 World Expo and was expecting 70 million visitors to the city during the six-month event. There were jobs available if we were prepared to stay.

I knew the words sounded familiar. 'Why would I want to leave all this?' I asked. How could I leave Shanghai? It had taken almost a year, but it had become our home. It was where the children had their friends and their *ayi*, whom they loved. I'd seen my family grow and adapt and thrive with opportunities and immersion in the

Chinese culture they would never have anywhere else. And I didn't want to leave. I'd only just got the hang of it.

It had been a hard slog to find our niche in Shanghai's bustling, pay-as-you-go, frenetic daily life. We had endured some really challenging times when our health in particular was put at risk due to where we lived. But we did live with a daily sense of excitement. The challenges hadn't worn us down, rather invigorated everyone in the family. Separately, we had all gained so much out of living in Shanghai. I'd seen Milly, who arrived when she was three and old enough to miss Australia, conquer feelings of home sickness and embrace a new life. She'd made wonderful new friends and was blossoming in her kindergarten where she was one of just seven children in the class and had a teacher with whom she had really clicked. It had taken a while but she had finally embraced the city and China and the language, though she was still not fussed on the food. She had taken a Chinese name, Mei Li (which means beautiful), that she was really proud of. She said it made her feel like one of the Chinese kids in her class. She could even write it in Chinese script.

Nelson couldn't wait to get out onto Shanghai's streets every day. There were so many cars and trucks and buses and motorbikes that he was invariably beside himself by the time the taxi pulled up to take us out in the morning. He would sit perched on my knee with his face up to the window counting in Mandarin the number of blue trucks he could see or using his Chinese to issue directions to the taxi driver to turn left, right or straight ahead. He'd turned from a toddler to a little boy in Shanghai and his world was the city. We had our little routines of playgroups and art sessions and singing, but we'd also wander the streets together talking about the people and the food and the noisy trucks. We'd look at the different buildings and houses and sneak into gardens and alleys to see what was going on and spot all the dragon and lion sculptures. He had an eye like an eagle for a Chinese flag and could smell a good dumpling a block away.

Smarty and I had never been tighter. There had been obviously special moments in China such as Smarty's proposal on the Great Wall. We cherished that our family was flourishing in the madcap flurry of making it through every day. We felt we were really living Shanghai at ground level, and making it work. There were no smooth, run-of-the-mill days. Even after all these months, living in Shanghai was like being trapped in sideshow alley. We'd go to bed each night buzzing with the excitement of what we'd achieved, and what we'd get to do tomorrow. It was the little things. It was having a whole conversation in stilted Mandarin, without having to resort to English. It was standing in the kitchen learning to make lunchtime pork dumplings in an assembly line with Milly under the direction of *ayi* Tina. It was braving a new local restaurant and coming out full and smiling. We'd eaten food we never thought we'd have tried in our lives and had children who were happy adding tofu, lotus root and seaweed to their diet – and asking for it in Chinese. We'd seen a city under snow, melting in the stifling summer heat and a city that boasted pockets of true beauty. We'd seen the old Shanghai and the new, and met young and old Chinese, all of whom were searching for their niche in China's future.

It was the peculiar scenarios that came with living in a foreign city with expats from around the world. It occurred to me that it

crime or misdemeanour began with the birthplace of the migrant responsible. After a particularly awful story about authorities intercepting a truckload of dogs that were destined for local restaurants, my editor expressed outrage at the suggestion people in Shanghai ate dog. While we were expecting a lecture on the tradition and reputation of Chinese cuisine, we soon realised her indignation was over the insinuation involving Shanghainese. 'People in Shanghai don't eat dog,' she said. 'It's those people in Guangzhou.'

The Shanghainese are also pushy, abrupt and very focused on seizing any opportunity to make money. While it was difficult to truly get to know many locals, we found our Shanghainese friends to be warm and funny and in possession of a complex view of their place in the world and what the next few years would hold for China.

What the next year would hold for us if we stayed in China, however, I did not know. As the financial crisis worsened, it seemed foolhardy to knock back the offer of a solid job that Smarty was keen on doing. Throwing our family's financial future into uncertainty because I loved living in Shanghai would have been selfish as would staying at the *Shanghai Daily*, which we no longer enjoyed, when an exciting new career opportunity beckoned. And so, we decided, we were going home.

Leaving was hard. Our shared experience with the joys and curve balls that came with living in Shanghai meant we had forged quick and strong friendships which we were sad to leave behind. Banding together to laugh at situations impossible to truly convey to people who just haven't lived in China made our fellow expats feel like family. Between farewell dinners and drinks, I also realised

I needed to do shopping. Lots of shopping. I had presents to buy, fake designer handbags to stock up on, clothes to have made and children's shoes to buy in about 10 different sizes. And I became obsessed with buying pulled-silk doonas.

I was after one of China's famous silk doonas for everyone in the family after a friend of mine described sleeping under the doona like floating in clouds. It sounded like the kind of night's sleep I might enjoy and a lasting memento of one of China's celebrated silk products. I'd heard of a massive local fabric market about an hour from the city centre which specialised in curtains and sheets and had stalls where they made silk doonas while you waited. I decided I just had to get to the market. But, like everything in Shanghai, that wasn't going to be easy. It was a major logistical task. I didn't want to take the children with me as it was such a long way in heavy city traffic and I wanted to be able to do my doona shopping without having to chase the pair of them through a thousand sheet shops. And I wanted *ayi* Tina with me. No-one at the market spoke English and, as I'd never really recovered from being ripped off at the Shanghai zoo in our first month when I was completely out of my element, I wanted to be armed with some local haggling expertise for my last tilt at picking up a bargain. When Smarty finished work, I took my chance. Bemused by being paid to take me shopping, Tina took charge. It was the one experience I'd missed in Shanghai. At last, I was being shown the city by a local.

Hidden way down the back of one the Qing Fang market's cavernous warehouses on Cao An Lu, far from the tourist-frequented zone of Shanghai, we found a silk doona stall. On a steel bed-sized table top, bundles of silk were being pulled and stretched by a team of women under the watchful eye of the store-owner who was armed with a pair of scales to ensure each doona weighed in with the right amount of silk. For layer after layer they pulled until the tiers of the silky fibres were piled high like stack of pancakes. Then they were wrapped into a doona cover, with the end result a blanket as soft and light as fairy floss. The process was fascinating, the doonas a delight. I ordered six.

In hindsight, adding six doonas to our luggage was not the best idea. Eventually, though, we packed away our Shanghai life and before we knew it were catching our last Chinese taxi out of the pre-dawn city to Pudong. I was a jumble of emotions on the flight to Australia. We'd left the bustle and winter freeze of Shanghai behind and landed in sunny Brisbane just as it lurched lazily into the long, hot Christmas holiday season. It was our home, but we felt foreign. Nothing seemed the same. After our year in Shanghai, Brisbane was just so bright.

We found ourselves back at Smarty's mum's house in suburban Brisbane where we'd stayed a year before while we were nervously preparing to board the plane to Shanghai. It was a typical Brisbane house with a verandah and a big back yard. The next morning, when we woke to realise we really were back in Australia, we took breakfast out on the verandah overlooking the expanse of green lawn that was interrupted only by the cement pathway to the clothes line and the garden shed. It was mowing day. As we sat there drinking water straight from the tap, eating unsoaked fruit and listening to the squark of a yardful of uncaged magpies, each of us was struck by the shredded green of the grass and the intense blue of the cloudless sky. We heard the strange, horn-free hum of the occasional passing car and smelled the sweetness of freshly cut grass mingled with the backyard frangipani. We sat there, all four of us, mesmerised for more than an hour. It was simple, it was beautiful, and we'd all missed it.

I'd also missed driving. It had been a year since I'd driven, but I was keen to get back behind the steering wheel and take on the leisurely holiday traffic. I had a specific outing in mind. I desperately wanted to get to the supermarket. With a wallet full of Australia's gaily-coloured dollars instead of yuan, I hit the nearest Woolworths. I must have looked a fool, standing at the entrance with my mouth agape. Everything just seemed so incredibly edible. I saw the familiar cartons of milk in the dairy display, comforting bread fresh from the bakery and vegetables I knew how to cook. I saw chocolate and eggs that I was sure wouldn't make us ill, cuts of meat that had helpful labels and cooking instructions, and boxes of cereal and cheese I could afford without taking out a loan. With a fright, I also saw the shoppers. If ever I doubted Australia was suffering from an obesity epidemic, this was my wake up call. People attached to protruding tummies and massive bottoms pushed trolleys piled high with produce up and down the aisles. Teens with flabby arms and muffin tops nibbled away on junk food while supersized families stocked up on Christmas treats. I hadn't seen a fat person in a year. They seemed to be ganging up on me on my return.

It was while I was standing at the deli display weighing up whether to opt for a low fat goat's cheese instead of a full-fat bocconcini to go with my semi-dried tomatoes that I ran into an old friend. I was so accustomed to being anonymous as I went about my business in the city that I was taken aback to bump into somebody who knew me. The boxes into which I'd bundled our China life hadn't yet arrived back in Australia so I'd had to don the only clean summer top I could find, which happened to be an 'I climbed the Great Wall of China' souvenir T-shirt. 'Have you really?' my friend Teresa asked pointing at my shirt, oblivious to all the experiences, dramas and changes I – and my family – had been through in the past year. 'Actually, I have,' I replied. 'It's really quite a story ...'

A NOTE FROM THE AUTHOR

Could it be possible to deeply miss a place so harsh, tricky, confusing and downright dirty as China? Could it really be culture shock that we felt coming home? Despite all the things we thought problematic about Shanghai, the difficulty of settling back into Australia caught me by surprise. It took many months for the quiet, the colour, the space and the cleanliness to seem right.

As a journalist writing this book, I expected everything to be easier after working within China's government-run media. But it wasn't so easy. I found out that researching and writing about China after my departure attracted wariness, closed doors and propaganda – this time from the West.

I remain indebted to the *Shanghai Daily* and the staff, especially Editor-in-Chief Peter Zhang, Editor JJ Jiang and Opinion Editor Wang Yong. I also credit the paper for many insights into the country and its people.

As well, I thank all of our dear Chinese and expat friends for the countless hours they subjected themselves to my pestering for their views on the big picture issues of China's place in the world. The Chinese block on Facebook and email did not thwart us.

It's my hope that this book offers some insight and understanding of the challenges and delights of Shanghai and China. My greatest lesson remains that while the world may be increasingly homogenous, East and West remain splendidly, and possibly permanently, immiscible.

It's also my hope that our story proves helpful for people making the decision to relocate abroad with family. The expat lifestyle phenomenon is becoming more common in many cities of the world.

This story is our personal snapshot, experience and impressions of Shanghai at a specific time. Our experience covered 2008. As it is China, much will have changed at the time of reading. Much will have stayed the same.